D1568570

MULTIMEDIA WEB DESIGN AND DEVELOPMENT

MULTIMEDIA WEB DESIGN AND DEVELOPMENT
Using Languages to Build Dynamic Web Pages

Theodor Richardson
Charles Thies

MERCURY LEARNING AND INFORMATION
Dulles, Virginia
Boston, Massachusetts
New Delhi

Publisher: David Pallai

MERCURY LEARNING AND INFORMATION
22841 Quicksilver Drive
Dulles, VA 20166
info@merclearning.com
www.merclearning.com
1-800-758-3756

This book is printed on acid-free paper.

Theodor Richardson and Charles Thies. *Multimedia Web Design and Development.*
ISBN: 978-1-936420-38-4

Library of Congress Control Number: 2012952664

131415 321

Printed in the United States of America

Our titles are available for adoption, license, or bulk purchase by institutions, corporations, etc. For additional information, please contact the Customer Service Dept. at 1-800-758-3756 (toll free).

I dedicate this book to Katherine; she is my muse and the love of my life. I would be lost without you, and everything in my life means more because you are in it.

— Theodor Richardson

To my sons, Matt and Will: Dream the impossible, learn from your mistakes, and try again. Hard work and perseverance will make all your dreams come true.

—Charles Thies

CONTENTS

Chapter 5
HTML5 123

Chapter 6
JAVASCRIPT AND JQUERY. 155

Introduction

This book is a complete guide to the concepts and practices of Web design and development. It includes hands-on activities and professional advice for best practices in learning the procedures and practices of both design and development, allowing you to practice the entire life cycle of a Web project. The material herein captures all of the stages, from initial designs to back-end programming, of creating complex Web applications. After completing this text, you will have the ability to create dynamic, engaging Web sites with interactive components and persistent styles. Each topic provides all of the necessary instruction for getting started in that particular area.

The first five chapters of the book focus on the front-end design of a Web site. This includes the use of HTML5 and CSS3 to create professional Web pages. This also includes guidelines for graphic design to make the most of your pages using color, font, and style. The professional tools Adobe Dreamweaver and Microsoft Expression Web are also introduced, with guidelines for their use in creating the case project that continues throughout the text.

Chapter 6 focuses on the use of JavaScript for creating dynamic elements and enabling interactions with the user. This also serves as an introduction to the common syntax for conditional statements, variable declarations, looping, and branching. This chapter completes the front-end development of the Web site and transitions into considerations for back-end Web application development. The jQuery library of functions for creating complex JavaScript effects across browsers is also introduced in this chapter, including instructions on installing the library to a site, linking it to a page, and implementing its functionality.

Chapter 7 introduces both PHP and Perl for developing back-end code for Web applications. It gives an overview of both programming languages, with the goal of focusing on common tasks needed for interactivity and processing user input through forms or JavaScript submissions. This chapter includes instructions for emailing from both of these server-side languages. In order to complete the activities for this chapter, you will need Web hosting that supports one or both of them. Ideally, the hosting solution you choose will also support MySQL for completing the case project in its entirety. GoDaddy.com basic hosting is recommended for this project, as it meets all of these criteria at a relatively low cost.

Chapter 8 introduces MySQL, the most commonly used open source database software, for data management and storage. This includes an introduction to databases and the SQL database language. The PHP toolkit is used for accessing, storing, and modifying data for use in a Web application. The case project is completed in this chapter with the storage and retrieval of information from the interactive form developed for the site.

Chapter Structure

Each chapter is structured so as to provide you with an overview and best practices for one component of creating a complete Web site from the front-end design to the back-end programming. The chapters contain hands-on activities both in the text and as standalone challenges to help you master the material. A case project is given as an example for you to follow and expand on. Two additional projects are presented to reinforce the material and allow you to practice it with different objectives. A knowledge check is provided to allow you to test your comprehension of the chapter. Answers to select odd-numbered questions are provided at the back of the book. Additional exercises and discussion questions are presented to help you further explore the concepts in each chapter.

Code Notation

Some lines of code are longer than the lines of text in this book. Whenever you see a ⏎ symbol in the code, the line immediately following it is a continuation that should be on the same line in your actual code. In HTML this is not important but in formal languages it is necessary to keep all of the code on the same line. The code snippets on the companion DVD contain the code in the correct lines for use.

Student Resource DVD

The textbook provides a DVD inside the back cover that includes resources and sample video tutorials for the student. This DVD includes all of the files needed to complete the chapter exercises within the text. You will also find a repository of high-resolution images from the chapters and companion Excel template documents for using common functions effectively. There are also student resources with additional project samples and videos for each chapter, as well as video tutorials, on the companion Web site for the book (*authorcloudware.com*).

Instructor Resource DVD

The instructor DVD contains the solutions for all of the exercises and knowledge checks, along with PowerPoint presentations for each chapter (*authorcloudware.com*).

Acknowledgments

Theodor Richardson:

I am very proud of the book that you now hold in your hands, and I want to thank you for choosing it over others. Web design has been a passion of mine and a profession for decades now, and I am pleased to share what I have learned with you. This book is the result of the combined creative forces of everyone who has worked to make it possible, and I want to offer my sincere thanks to them all, whether we have met or not. I want to thank Katie Kennedy for her continued support, patience, and understanding as well as for her unprecedented ability to make café lattes instantly as needed. I also want to thank my grandparents, Leonard and Sylvia Ullom, and my parents, Dan and Deborah Richardson, for giving me such a wonderful upbringing and perpetual support and for helping me to capitalize on the opportunities that have led to my lifelong dream of seeing a book of my own creation in print. I would like to thank my publisher, David Pallai, and my co-author and friend, Charles Thies, for seeing another project through to completion. Last, and certainly not least, I want to thank you, dear reader, for your support.

Charles Thies:

I certainly have many people to thank who have made this project possible. We have been writing now for a couple of years, and I would like to thank my beautiful wife, Lea, and my sons, Matt and Will, for their patience and support throughout. I would like to extend a special thank you to my friend and co-author, Ted, for all of his guidance and support throughout the project. A very special thank you to all of the people we know worked to make this textbook possible but we never met. Finally, a very special thank you to the students and professors who have adopted this book; you are the reason we are always thinking about new ways to present material in the best format so that you will be prepared in your field of study.

Web Design Basics

This chapter presents an introduction to the basic concepts of Web design. This includes an introduction to the World Wide Web (WWW), including a brief history and an overview of how resources can be interlinked via a Uniform Resource Locator (URL). You will also start to practice creating and opening HTML files, the basis of the interconnectivity of the World Wide Web, and explore some preliminary designs for the two core projects of the text, as well as principles that you can use for your own projects later. Once you have completed this chapter, you should be able to:

- Discuss the history of the World Wide Web

- Identify the components of a URL and understand interlinking of Web documents

- Construct a new HTML document and open it in a Web browser

- Create a preliminary design for your Web site

1.1 INTRODUCTION TO THE WORLD WIDE WEB

The Internet is a vast interconnection of networks that spans the world and allows computers to communicate from any point on the globe to any other point on the globe that shares a connection to this vast complex network. The Internet of today grew from an initial interconnection of United States government servers under a project called ARPANET and has expanded across the globe. From the user perspective, the Internet is most recognizable from the services that it offers; these services prominently include e-mail and the World Wide Web.

The **Internet** is a global interconnection of networks made up of hardware devices, such as personal computers and servers, which supports communication between different computing devices using an addressing scheme known as Internet Protocol (IP).

The **World Wide Web (or Web)** is a service that runs on the Internet to provide access to documents, audio, and video and allows the interconnection of these documents through the use of hyperlinks.

The World Wide Web (commonly abbreviated as "the Web") is a service that runs on the Internet to allow users with an Internet connection to access publicly available documents that are shared by organizations and individuals. It is the most common application on the Internet and is most likely what people have in mind when they think of the Internet.

In the 1980s and 1990s, Tim Berners-Lee, a physicist working as a contractor at CERN (Conseil Européen pour la Recherche Nucléaire, which translated from French means European Organization for Nuclear Research), developed what is now known as the World Wide Web through a variety of projects. Berners-Lee had a grand vision for a system that could link information through a "web" of interconnections between documents across different computers.

These interconnections between resources were called *hyperlinks* and acted as a way of managing and sharing information among individual nodes, documents, and machines. The hyperlinked documents contained text and hyperlinks and became known as hypertext documents; this is the same as a *Web page* today, though they have become much more sophisticated and have integrated a number of other scripting and programming languages and technologies.

Tim Berners-Lee developed the Hypertext Transfer Protocol (HTTP), which would essentially allow a user to click on one of these hyperlinks to easily move from one hypertext document (or later, Web page) to another using an interpreter program that is called a *Web browser*; the early Web browser that he wrote was called *WorldWideWeb*.

This system allowed resources to be accessed by remote machines that were interconnected via shared network protocols. Using the backbone of the Internet, HTTP and the resource access and hyperlinking it enables have allowed the Web to expand into daily use on desktop computers, servers, laptops, and mobile devices. Web pages are individual documents that are stored on Web-enabled servers (or Web servers), which contain hyperlinks to other Web pages, documents, and applications. A set of interrelated Web pages is called a *Web site*.

As the power of computers has grown, Web browsers have expanded in capability from simple document retrieval and display to media-rich interfaces that can act as robustly as a standalone application installed on a computer. However, the core principles of this system remain and will be the focus of this first chapter.

A **Web site** is a collection of Web pages, documents, audio, and video that is stored in a location such as a Web server and can be accessed by a unique address determined by a Uniform Resource Locator (URL) value.

A **Web server** is a repository that contains all of the files and folders for a Web site and provides remote access to them via various protocols such as HTTP and File Transfer Protocol (FTP), over the Internet.

A **Web browser** is a software application used to search, navigate, and retrieve information and data from the Web.

1.1.1 Web Pages and Web Browsers

A Web page is a document designed for interpretation in a specialized application called a Web browser. Modern Web pages have evolved from the simple concept of linking text documents to each other via hyperlinks to an interrelated set of scripting and programming languages that operate to provide a complex display capable of providing rich, media-driven experiences for a user. Web pages use a base language called Hypertext Markup Language (HTML), which provides a means of complex media display and delivery along with simple text inclusion. The file type of a Web page is *.htm* or *.html*.

A Web browser is a user application that retrieves Web pages and interprets them for display on a user's machine. The Web browser display is known as a WYSIWYG display, for "What You See Is What You Get"; each Web browser will interpret the HTML code differently, so content may not display the same way on different browsers. There are a variety of Web browsers available for use.

Because of the differences in display, the World Wide Web Consortium (W3C) has set standards of behavior and display for Web-based languages such as HTML and Cascading Style Sheets (CSS). You should bookmark **www. w3c.org** on your most commonly used Web browser as a reference for usage whenever you are in doubt about the behavior and application of a Web-based language component.

The most common Web browsers in use today are Microsoft Internet Explorer, Mozilla Firefox, Google Chrome, and Apple Safari. The global statistics on browser use (as determined by *statowl.com*) can be seen in Figure 1.1. The use of the different browsers varies by region. Internet Explorer is the primary browser used in North America, whereas Google Chrome has the largest use in Asia. Mozilla Firefox is the most used browser in Europe. Apple Safari has seen increased usage in recent years because of its integration with the Apple iPad.

At this point, it is safe to assume that supporting Internet Explorer, Mozilla Firefox, Google Chrome, and Apple Safari will allow your site to reach nearly any audience set you desire.

The four most common browsers can be downloaded for free. It is recommended that you

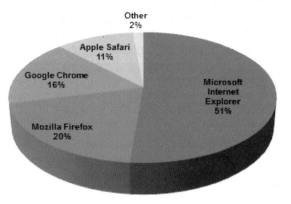

Global Web Browser Usage

▲ **FIGURE 1.1** Global Browser Usage Statistics

have at least three of them installed on your computer for testing purposes as you begin to design and develop more complex Web pages and applications. The most common Web browsers can be downloaded from the following sites:

ACTIVITY 1.1 – WEB BROWSER INSTALLATION AND UPDATING

As you go further in the chapter, you will start to plan two course projects. You will need to test these on multiple Web browsers to ensure compatibility. To prepare for this, you should make sure you have at least Internet Explorer (www. microsoft.com) and Firefox (www.firefox.com) on a Windows machine and Safari (www.apple.com/safari) and Firefox (www.firefox.com) on a Mac OS machine. You can use the indicated homepages for each of these software tools to download the respective software or update the Web browsers you already have installed to the latest version.

- **Microsoft Internet Explorer (IE):** This browser is a Windows OS–exclusive browser designed to integrate more fully with the Windows desktop environment. IE contains ActiveX technology, which can allow it to function in a more robust manner and provide greater depth of content on Windows machines; scripting for ActiveX requires separate considerations from those of normal Web design and development for general use. IE can be downloaded from the Microsoft homepage at *www.microsoft.com*.

- **Mozilla Firefox:** This browser is compatible with the Windows, Mac OS, and Linux operating systems, as well as some mobile devices (as an app). It can be downloaded from the homepage *www.firefox.com*.

- **Google Chrome:** Chrome is a browser that has recently gained market share. It is compatible with multiple operating systems and integrates with Google's other online services, such as Google Docs. It can be downloaded from *www.google.com/chrome*.

- **Apple Safari:** Safari is the default browser for Mac OS and is directly integrated with Apple iOS devices, including the iPad. A version of Safari is also available for Windows. You can download Safari from *www.apple.com/safari*.

One of the browsers you should seriously consider having on your computer for testing is Mozilla Firefox. It includes a Web Developer tool (accessible directly from the Firefox main menu), which will assist you in evaluating your HTML code, CSS commands, and JavaScript execution. If you are unsure why your page is not working or displaying properly, opening it in Firefox and using the Web Developer tools Web Console and Error Console can save you a significant amount of time debugging your page or application.

1.12 Hypertext Markup Language (HTML)

A Web page is written in the language of the Web, Hypertext Markup Language (HTML). HTML files are made up of text and formatting commands called tags. The tags of HTML can be used to format the text in the page and to establish page structure. Without any tags, HTML pages act like continuous lines of text, breaking at the boundaries of the Web browser window. (This is similar to their behavior in text editors like Microsoft Word when no formatting is applied). The HTML tags allow this flow to be changed and formatted to create complex pages with clearly delineated visual elements.

HTML 5 has deviated from strict adherence to SGML, but the tags and rules that have carried over from prior versions of HTML (such as HTML 4.01) still operate under SGML rules and constraints. This deviation in structure will be covered in later chapters, but you should concentrate on structured HTML to help you learn good habits as you begin using the language.

HTML is a highly structured language. Its rules and form are defined by the structure of its parent language, Standard Generalized Markup Language (SGML). HTML is a sister language to eXtensible Markup Language (XML), which is used for data transmission and interoperability. This is the reason for the commonality in tag format between HTML and XML. You can see this hierarchy visually in Figure 1.2.

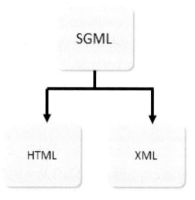

▲ **FIGURE 1.2** Hierarchy of Markup Languages

The tags in HTML are signified by angle brackets (the less than and greater than symbols) wrapping the name of the tag, such as *<title>* to signify the title tag. You can view tags in HTML as on and off switches. Anything that is turned on must be turned off. To turn off a tag, you would use a slash before the name of the tag between the less than and greater than symbols, such as *</title>* to signify the end of the title. Any text included between the initialization tag and the end tag will be formatted according to the behavior of the tag. For example, the HTML code *<title>My Page</title>* would make the page title "My Page" in the Web browser in which it is displayed. HTML is interpreted by the browser, and the application of the tags for formatting the document depends upon their placement in the page. You will discover the rules and specifics of HTML tags as you continue through the text.

HTML is case insensitive, so the tag <TiTLE> and the tag <title> will behave in the same manner. But according to W3C, the HTML tag names should always be in lowercase letters, so that is the convention you should adopt.

1.1.3 Uniform Resource Locator (URL)

Web resources are identified by a Uniform Resource Locator (URL). This is a pathway that establishes the server and file that the Web browser is attempting to access on behalf of the user. You can see a sample breakdown of the pieces of a URL in Figure 1.3. The URL is entered into the address bar of the Web browser to establish a connection to the specified resource. URLs cannot include blank spaces (Whenever you see "%20" in a URL, it is the browser attempting to reconcile a blank space in the path.)

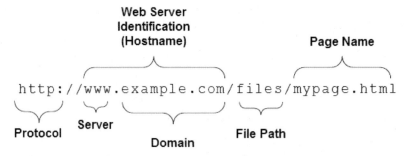

▲ FIGURE 1.3 Example Breakdown of a URL

The individual pieces of the URL

http://www.example.com/files/mypage.html are as follows:

- First, **http** is the protocol. A protocol is a set of messages coupled together to transmit information in a way that both the sender and receiver can understand. The common protocols you may see for Web use are *http* (used for connecting to a Web resource), *https* (the secure version of HTTP), *ftp* (File Transfer Protocol, used for uploading and downloading files), and *mailto* (used to invoke the default e-mail program).

- Next, the colon *(:)* separates the protocol from the input command. The input command is the rest of the URL information after the colon.

- The two slashes (*//*) signify that contact to a server should be established.

- The next section is the Web server identification (which is also called the hostname); in this case it is *www.example.com*. This specifies a unique Web server to which the Web browser will submit a resource request. Alternatively, you may see a set of numbers separated by period characters, such as *128.163.1.1;* this also uniquely identifies a server by its Internet Protocol (IP) address. The humanly readable text is a convenience for users that connects to a numerical server address.

- Within the Web server identification, the **www** signifies the server that should be listening for a request from the protocol. The *www* can be omitted in almost all cases because it will be assumed by default. Other text may precede the domain name, representing subdomains (such as *videos.example.com,* in which *videos* is the subdomain).

- The text **example.com** is the domain name. This is uniquely bound to a preset folder on a Web server by whoever owns the domain.

- The text **com** is the Top-Level Domain (TLD), the top level in the domain hierarchy; it assists in uniquely identifying server names. There are only a limited number of these in existence, though more are being created as the old ones are exhausted. Common TLD names include *com* (for commercial use), *org* (typically for non-profit organizations), *edu* (for educational use), and *gov* (for government Web sites).

- The rest of the address is used to locate local resources on the specified Web server. The **files** portion of the address represents the file structure (called the file path) beyond the main folder of the location within the Web server. Multiple subfolders can be identified as part of the file path (such as *media/videos,* in which *videos* is a subfolder of *media* and the *media* folder resides in the main folder identified for the Web server identification).

- The final portion of the URL is the filename. In this case, it is **mypage.html**. This identifies the specific resource that the Web browser is requesting from the Web server. Most of these filenames will be HTML files with an extension of *.htm* or *.html*.

When there is no filename specified, the server will look for either index.htm or index.html. For this reason, you should always name the homepage of your site either index.htm or index.html so the server can find it immediately with a reference to the containing folder. This will be reiterated throughout the project planning, but you should make note of it now.

1.2 HTML PAGE CONSTRUCTION

HTML pages are written in text, and they act the same way no matter which program is used to write them. You will experience some of the different design tool options in the next chapter, but no matter which one you choose, the code that results will be the same format and can be opened in any Web authoring or text processing program. The simplest program to use when writing HTML is a plain text editor, like Notepad on Windows or TextEdit for Mac OS. Any program that saves plain text files (as .txt) can be used to create an HTML document.

More complex word processing programs, like Microsoft Word, can create HTML, but their use is not recommended. You must be careful with how you save your files on these programs to avoid formatting code in your document in a language other than HTML and extraneous code added by the editor. You should make sure that the Type field of the Save As dialog box says either "Text" or "Plain Text" before you complete the save operation.

Every HTML page has the same basic structure. It includes an initial <html> tag to signify that HTML formatting rules should be applied by the browser; this must be turned off at the end of the page with an </html> tag to close the document content. Inside the HTML page are two main parts, the head and the body.

The recommended text editor to use for HTML creation is Notepad++; it runs on any operating system and can be downloaded (for free) either as an executable file or as source files that can be compiled for your specific machine. The benefit of this program is that it identifies tags in your document with highlighting after you have saved the page with an HTML extension (either .htm or .html). It can also identify code in other programming languages, such as JavaScript and PHP, which you will use as you start to develop more complex Web pages and Web sites. Even when you start using design tools for your HTML pages, Notepad++ is a beneficial tool for editing and error-checking HTML and embedded code. Notepad++ is available from the Web site notepad-plus-plus.org.

The head is signified by the <head> tag and closed by the </head> tag. This section is used for configuration information and non-displaying elements. The only portion of the head that displays in the browser is the title. This is where you will place your CSS styles and interlink external resources as you add complexity to your pages.

The body is signified by the <body> tag, which should be placed after the closing </head> tag. The body is where all of the content should be placed that you want to display in the browser window. The body must also be closed with </body> before you close the HTML tag with </html>.

ACTIVITY 1.2 – CREATING A TEMPLATE PAGE AND PROJECT FOLDER

For this activity, you will create a folder to house your projects for this textbook and create a template file for your HTML pages. First, choose a location on your computer and create a new folder called "WebProjects" (with no spaces in the name; you should not include spaces in any folder or filenames used for the Web). You will create new folders inside of this folder for the activities and projects throughout this text. Housing everything in the same folder structure will help you when linking documents together and invoking resources within your pages.

Using the page outline given below, open a text editor and type the page structure into it, from the <html> tag to the </html> tag. You should save this file as template.html inside the WebProjects folder. This will allow you to create a new page by opening this file without the need to retype this structure. You should follow along with the remaining parts of this chapter to expand your template file to include the additional elements needed.

The complete structure for an HTML page with the head and body elements included is as follows:

```
<html>
    <head>

    </head>
    <body>

    </body>
</html>
```

You can use this as a guide for placing your content and resources. There are additional elements that are common to all HTML pages that you will explore in the next few sections. These include the document type (doctype) declaration and page title.

1.2.1 The Doctype Declaration

A Doctype Declaration (DTD) is an instruction to the browser specifying the type of content the browser will encounter in the page. The need for a DTD is based on the different versions of HTML that can be used in a page and the widespread inclusion of XML documents on the Web. A DTD tells the browser how to interpret what follows in the page.

 Some Web browsers are more forgiving of errors than others. For example, Firefox allows you to open a page that does not include a DTD, but you should never depend on this forgiveness, as it can cause compatibility issues in other browsers.

There are a variety of DTD values that you may encounter, but the two DTDs you will likely need to use most often are for HTML 5 and HTML 4.01. Eventually, you should construct all of your pages in HTML 5. The command for a DTD is <!DOCTYPE>; this is in upper case because it is a browser instruction, not an HTML tag.

The DTD you should use for HTML 4.01 is:

```
<!DOCTYPE HTML PUBLIC "-//W3C//DTD HTML 4.01 Transi-
tional//EN" "http://www.w3.org/TR/html4/loose.dtd">
```

There are different DTDs for HTML 4.01, but the "loose" specification from the example is more forgiving and allows the use of presentational content and deprecated tags (tags that were once part of the standard but have been retired). Ideally, you would use the strict DTD, but it is more difficult to determine errors as a beginner, since the errors may simply be omitted from the browser content. The words and strings (denoted by quotation marks) following the word DOCTYPE inside the tag are called attributes; you will encounter attributes frequently as you expand your understanding of HTML. Attributes are always separated from the tag name by a blank space.

The DTD for HTML 5 is simpler, because it is not a derivative of SGML. The DTD for HTML 5 is as follows:

```
<!DOCTYPE html>
```

The DTD tag for a page does not have an end tag like most HTML tags and does not have to be closed. These tags are also case insensitive, like other HTML tags, but convention dictates that they should be capitalized. The page structure with an HTML 5 DTD is as follows:

```
<!DOCTYPE html>
<html>
    <head>

    </head>
    <body>

    </body>
</html>
```

ACTIVITY 1.3 – ADDING DTDS TO THE TEMPLATE PAGE

For this activity, you should open template.html in the text editor of your choice and add a DTD declaration before the <html> tag. Be sure to save your file when you are finished.

1.2.2 Adding a Title

The next element that should always be included in an HTML page is a title. A title is added inside the head using the <title> and </title> tags. Whatever text is typed between the opening and closing tags will be treated as the page title by the browser. For instance, to call a page "My Page Title," you would use the following code inside the head of the file:

```
<title>My Page Title</title>
```

The complete code for the page with a title included is:

```
<!DOCTYPE html>
<html>
    <head>
    <title>My Page Title</title>
    </head>
    <body>

    </body>
</html>
```

ACTIVITY 1.4 – ADDING A TITLE

For this activity, you will add a placeholder for your page title in your template.html file. Make sure you place the <title> and </title> tags within the head of the HTML document. You can use "My Page Title" as your placeholder value, but you will need to change this for each page you create. Be sure to save your file when you are finished.

1.2.3 Adding Content

The content of your page that you want to display in the main window of the Web browser is placed inside of the body (between the <body> and </body> tags). You can type plain text in this area and it will display in the Web browser window using the default font and format for the browser. Without any formatting, the text may appear differently on different browsers. Almost all of your page development will be for the body of the document, since this is what your audience will see. Only the title, meta information about the page, JavaScript code and CSS formatting will be placed inside the head of the document.

ACTIVITY 1.5 – HELLO, WORLD!

One of the first programming activities in any language is to create a program to print the text "Hello, World!" on the screen. This has become a computing tradition that you will continue in this activity. Fortunately, displaying text is very simple once you have the HTML page structure complete. For this activity, you should open the template.html file in a text editor and save the file as hello.html inside the WebProjects folder. Change the title of your HTML page (the content between <title> and </title>) to the text "Hello, World!" and add the text "Hello, World!" to the page inside the body of the document (between the <body> and </body> tags).

1.2.4 Adding a Hyperlink

One of the key features of using hypertext is the ability to link a document to other resources and documents. To do this, you can create a hyperlink (or link) inside your HTML document. The tag that you will use to create this link is the anchor tag, denoted <a> in HTML. Link text will (by default) be colored blue and underlined. You can see an example of linked text compared to regular text in Figure 1.4.

The text between the opening <a> tag and the closing </a> tag will be the highlighted text that appears in the browser window. For example, in Figure 1.4, the text between the <a> and </a> tags is "This is a link."

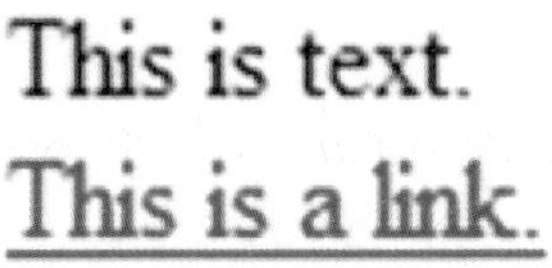

This is text.
This is a link.

▲ **FIGURE 1.4** Linked Text

In order to set a destination for the link (the resource to which the Web browser will connect when the link is clicked by the user), you must use an attribute inside of the <a> tag. This attribute is the hyper-reference attribute, abbreviated *href*. The attribute *href* requires a value; this creates what is called an attribute/value pair. The code for this is:

```
<a href="destination">This is a link.</a>
```

The text "This is a link." can be changed to any text. Similarly, the text "destination" should be replaced with the actual URL of the resource that is to be accessed. There are two types of URL referencing that are accepted by the *href* attribute:

- **Global Referencing:** This type of reference specifies the complete URL for a resource. For example, you could link to the Google homepage with the following code:

```
<a href="http://www.google.com">Google HomePage</a>
```

- **Relative Referencing:** This type of reference specifies a resource based on its location relative to the current page. For example, if you had two pages in the same folder named *page1.html* and *page2.html,* then you could link to *page2.html* inside *page1.html* with the following code:

```
<a href="page2.html">Page 2</a>
```

You do not have to add any attributes to a closing tag; all of the attribute/value pairs should be contained in the opening tag.

1.2.5 Page Testing

Once you have made changes to an HTML page or created a new one, it is always a good idea to test it in a Web browser. If you have a default Web browser set for your computer, the easiest way to test the document is to double-click the icon inside of the WebProjects folder. Since the document type is HTML, it will open in a Web browser instead of a text editor. If you do not have a default Web browser set for your computer or you wish to test the file in a different browser, you can right-click the icon and select *Open with* and choose the browser you want to use to open the file.

In Firefox, you can select the Firefox menu, choose **New Tab**, and then choose **Open File** to select an HTML file you want to open on your local computer.

The browser will interpret the page content for display and show it in the browser window. You can see an example of this in Figure 1.5 for the *hello.html* page you have created through the activities in this chapter. You should open this file in your own Web browser of choice to see how the results of your work are interpreted.

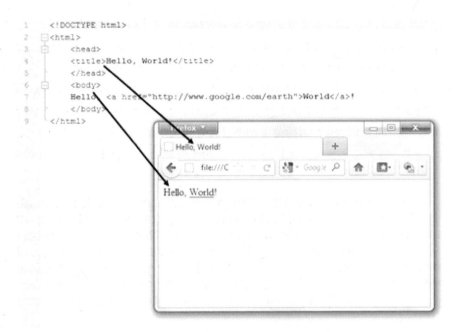

```
1    <!DOCTYPE html>
2    <html>
3        <head>
4        <title>Hello, World!</title>
5        </head>
6        <body>
7        Hello <a href="http://www.google.com/earth">World</a>!
8        </body>
9    </html>
```

▲ **FIGURE 1.5** Testing an HTML Page

From the figure, you can see where the different elements of the page translate in the browser. The title of the page will be located in the top part of the browser interface. The main browser window is where the body of the page is displayed. The address bar will display the URL of the file. In this case, it will begin with *file://C:*, because it is using local file access on the C drive of your machine. (A different letter may display if you have selected a different default storage drive.)

1.3 PRINCIPLES OF WEB DESIGN

Now that you have an understanding of the basic mechanics of constructing and testing a page, you should pause to consider how you will design and structure your HTML pages individually or for an entire Web site. When you create pages for the Web, you are creating a complete visual interface that is more dynamic than print and more interactive than slides or videos. You need to keep this interactivity in mind and consider the flow of information through your page. There are basic principles you should consider for even small projects and individual pages of content. Applying these will ensure that you construct an appealing presentation for your viewers, which is one of the most critical aspects of creating effective Web pages.

1.3.1 Page Layout and Real Estate

By default, the content of a Web page will display from left to right in a continuous line until it hits the end of the browser window, at which point it will continue in the next line down back at the left margin. There are techniques for dividing up the page into more manageable sections (such as using tables and using positioning style commands). When you consider where elements should be placed on your page, you should consider the importance of the location on the page (commonly called "real estate") where you will place them.

The upper left-hand corner is considered your most valuable real estate. This is the portion of the page that the viewer will see first, which is why it is considered the most valuable. This is also the reason most logos are placed in the upper left-hand corner of a Web page. Above all, you want your viewer to be able to identify the site and its ownership on sight. There is no set demarcation for the primary real estate of a page, but you should not assume it extends further than 25% of the horizontal or vertical space of the page.

According to W3C, the common browser display size is now 1024 pixels by 768 pixels. This means you can plan a site for this size and assume that 98% of your viewing audience will be able to see the site in a single window without scrolling.

The secondary real estate of a page extends in two directions. Anything to the right of the primary real estate is considered secondary real estate. This is because most viewers will be able to see this space without scrolling, which makes it second only to the upper left-hand corner for visibility and accessibility.

The other area of secondary real estate is from the bottom left-hand corner of the browser window up to the primary real estate. The entire left-hand side is not considered secondary real estate, because part of it may not be visible without scrolling. When you plan your site, you want to make sure any left-hand menu content does not require the user to scroll down on the page, or they will likely not see those menu items.

Users will not scroll a page unless they are vested in it by interest in something it contains. There is almost no possibility of their finding content hidden past the standard browser size of the page unless it is related directly to content presented on the visible part of the page that prompts them to explore further. You always want to make sure your menu and branding information fit within the standard browser size, so you do not have to rely on user scrolling and exploration for them to be able to navigate through your site.

The space beyond these two areas is what is typically designated for the content of the page. This is the tertiary real estate. In a complete Web site, this is the only area that should be altered from page to page, in order to establish consistency. Additionally, you should not require a user to scroll down on the page more than once (if at all). Users are unlikely to scroll more than once on a page and remain on the page. You can see a complete breakdown of these regions of a Web page in Figure 1.6.

▲ **FIGURE 1.6** Real Estate of a Web Page

Considering Purpose and Audience

The two most important aspects to consider when creating either a single page or a complete Web site are the purpose of the site and the intended audience. These two elements will vary drastically by project, but establishing them early will prevent you from having to redesign the site later.

The purpose of your site is something you should be able to summarize in one sentence at most. This should be your key idea behind every decision later in constructing the site. For a personal site that advertises your skills and history, the purpose may be "to showcase your skills and accomplishments in a visually interesting way." You can then ask design questions against this core goal. For instance, if there is an element you are not sure you should include, you can ask, "Does this element showcase my skills and accomplishments in a visually interesting way?" If the answer is yes, then it should be kept. If not, you need to rethink how to integrate that information or whether to include it at all.

The audience is another essential consideration. You should determine who will be viewing the site and what impression you want to give them. For instance, a military site filled with cartoon characters and bright colors will likely not be taken very seriously. Similarly, a site intended for children that contains nothing but black text on a white background will not grab the attention of your audience and will likely never be viewed again. You have to consider the tone of your site when deciding how to present your content. Knowing the audience you wish to address should help to set that tone. The question you can use to test your design ideas against your audience is "Will my audience react well to this design element?" According to research done by the Stanford Web Credibility Project, the professionalism and coherence of a site are among the most influential factors in a user's believing in the credibility of the site and its content.

1.3.3 Typography and Font Selection

Typography is the process of arranging letters in a specific arrangement to make language readable. This was once a specialized occupation, but with the advent of personal computing, typography is something in which everyone who types a document participates. The typeface, size, and spacing of the letters are all contributing factors in typography; these are all choices that are made in composing any visual document, including Web pages.

A typeface is a collection of symbols that form an alphabet; each typeface has its own unique style of display, such as the typefaces Times New Roman and Arial, two common typefaces installed on most machines. It is very likely that you will see *typeface* confused with the term *font* (as in the case of CSS), since they are almost synonymous. A font is actually a combination of a typeface and a size, so 10-point Arial is a font. With the advent of digital typography, the selection of a font is typically separate from the sizing, making the choice of typeface and that of the font virtually indistinguishable.

A **font** is a typeface combined with a set size, such as 10pt Arial. In most modern computing systems, fonts allow size modifications, so the terms "typeface" and "font" are becoming synonymous.

A **serif** is a decoration on a letter of text. This is a nonessential element that graphically enhances a character without adding any new information; these are used mostly to enhance readability by distinguishing the letters from each other and for artistic effect.

Monospacing in terms of typing is the characteristic of having all letters typed occupying the same amount of horizontal space regardless of the inherent letter size.

There are two major classifications of fonts: serif and sans-serif. A *serif* is a text decoration added to letters of the font, such as you would find in Times New Roman. Sans-serif means a font without these text decorations present. You can see examples of both types of fonts in Figure 1.7.

Times New Roman – serif
Batang – serif
Jokerman – serif

Arial – sans-serif
Dotum– sans-serif
Verdana – sans-serif

▲ **FIGURE 1.7** Examples of Serif and Sans-Serif Fonts

The font is also determined by the size of the text. Most modern fonts accommodate multiple sizes with the same display. A pixel is the smallest unit of display on your computer monitor; the standard resolution for a computer is 72 pixels per inch. In the world of type-setting, there are 72 *points* per inch, meaning that a point is roughly equivalent to a pixel on the screen. Therefore, a 12-point (abbreviated *12pt*) font would occupy roughly 12 pixels of space on a digital display. A less common measurement you may see is a pica; a pica is equivalent to 12 points. Pica rulers are most common in desktop publishing applications.

There are two types of spacing available in the design of fonts: monospacing and proportional spacing. In monospacing, all of the characters in the font occupy the same horizontal width when typed; this was the common case for most fonts in mechanical typewriters, since the motion of the typing carriage was fixed. Proportional spacing, on the other hand, allows letters to occupy only the space each one needs to display.

The spacing between adjacent letters in a font is also established by default, but you can adjust this manually; this process of adjustment is called kerning. Adjusting the spacing between words is called tracking. The spacing between lines (which is typically part of paragraph formatting) is called leading. Most of these parameters can be adjusted using style commands (via Cascading Style Sheets [CSS]).

The choice of font for a project varies greatly. With the variety of fonts available from which to choose, it is a matter of creative choice. However, as a general rule of design, you should have no more than two fonts occupying the same page, a primary font and a secondary font. More than this makes the arrangement look haphazard and poorly planned. You can use different sizes of each font on the page to add emphasis with size variation.

There are a variety of typefaces or fonts that come installed on any modern computer system, but not all of these are common to every machine. The Web browser uses the computer's installed fonts to visualize the page, so if a user does not have a font installed because it is uncommon, your page will not look the way you designed it. It is possible (through style commands) to select multiple fonts, so you have a backup if your first choice of font is not installed on the user's computer, but you should restrict your font choices to commonly installed fonts like Arial, Helvetica, Times New Roman, and Courier New. If you need a unique font to complete the look of your page, you should consider placing it inside an image, so it remains constant whether the font is installed on the user's machine or not.

1.3.4 Color Choice

Color choice in a page is as essential as the content. Color carries a significant amount of visual information that is consciously and subconsciously interpreted by the viewer. You should always limit your color palette for the design of a page or site. (This does not include photographs and videos included in the site.)

A good way to evaluate your color choice for a page is to view the colors adjacent to each other to test for contrast and conflict. As you become more proficient with design, you can create a table and set the background color of each cell to one of the colors you want to use and see how they interact. This will be revisited later, but it is something you should start to consider now.

A general guideline to use is to have two main colors and an accent color. You can use different shades of the main colors, and the two main colors should blend well together. The accent color should be used sparingly, and it should provide enough contrast to be readable over both of the main colors. You can see a map of complementary and analogous colors on the color wheel in Figure 1.8.

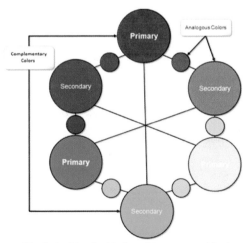

▲ FIGURE 1.8 The Color Wheel, with Complementary and Analogous Colors

There are an almost endless number of usable color combinations, but using two analogous colors and a complementary color for one of them is usually a safe way to construct your palette. You can also use the Web to research standard color palettes, but you need to make sure you have a limited number of colors, or your page will appear cluttered and unorganized. You should make sure that any text you include is readable above all else and that the tension between the colors does not draw attention away from the content; you can lighten or darken any of the colors to enhance or decrease the contrast presented. Remember, the more contrast you have between your text and the background, the clearer your text will be.

One color you should avoid is pure red; it is incredibly difficult for a person to look at pure red on a computer screen for any sustained period of time. If you want to verify this, you can open your template.html page and save it as red.html. Inside the body tag, add the attribute/value pair bgcolor="red" and change the title to "Red." The code for the <body> tag should be the following:

```
<body bgcolor="red">
```

Now save the page and open it in a Web browser. How long can you look at the page before you have to turn away or close it?

When choosing the colors for your pages or site, you should consider the emotional association that people have with colors. There is some variation in this in different cultures (such as traditional black for mourning in the Western world and traditional white for mourning in the Eastern world), and context plays a significant role, but Figure 1.9 will give you a starting point to research the colors you want to use and associate them with the message you want to convey.

Color	Emotional Associations
White	Clean, Open, Pure
Black	Dark, Serious, Formal, Powerful
Yellow	Happy, Energetic
Orange	Anxious, Warm, Energetic
Red	Irritated, Angry, Desirous
Purple	Royal, Feminine, Bored
Blue	Calm, Stable, Cold
Green	Young, Healthy, Content

▲ **FIGURE 1.9** Color and Emotion

1.3.5 Evaluating Existing Design for Tone

One of the best methods of learning to establish the right tone for your Web projects is to evaluate the sites you use on a regular basis for their tone and alignment with their intended purpose and audience. As you traverse the Web, you will start to see elements that do not work effectively or that disrupt the flow of a page. You may also find sites that do not have consistency across pages. These should begin to influence your own design decisions; knowing what works and what does not work will allow you to better align your own sites to their intended purpose and audience.

ACTIVITY 1.7: WEB SITE EVALUATIONS

For this activity, you should find five Web sites that effectively align their presentation with their purpose and audience and five Web sites that do not. For each site, record at least two things that the site designers did right or wrong, depending on the category to which you assign them.

CHAPTER SUMMARY

This chapter introduced you to the fundamental structure and history of HTML, the language of the Web. HTML can be written in any text editor, because it is a combination of plain text and formatting. Every HTML page should contain a Doctype Declaration (DTD), a head, and a body. The head of the page is used for configuration information and references to external resources. The body of the page is what is displayed in the Web browser when the page is accessed via its Uniform Resource Locator (URL). The Web presents a unique environment that can deliver rich and interactive media experiences. The fundamental elements that should guide the development of Web pages are a clear purpose and target audience. The tone of the site will be established through font and color choices. The next chapter will cover site planning and the professional HTML creation tools available on the market.

CHAPTER KNOWLEDGE CHECK

1 Which of the following document elements does not reside between the <html> and </html> tags?

- ○ **A.** head
- ○ **B.** body
- ○ **C.** title
- ○ **D.** doctype
- ○ **E.** None of the above

2 Which of the following is not part of a URL?

- ○ **A.** Protocol
- ○ **B.** Hostname
- ○ **C.** Filename
- ○ **D.** File path
- ○ **E.** None of the above

3

By technical definition, a font is an associated _____ and a_____.

- ○ **A.** Family, kerning
- ○ **B.** Typeface, kerning
- ○ **C.** Typeface, size
- ○ **D.** Family, size

4

Which of the following is a sibling language of HTML?

- ○ **A.** SGML
- ○ **B.** XML
- ○ **C.** XHTML
- ○ **D.** VBML

5

Which of the following retains the largest global market share of Web browsers in use, according to research by *statowl.com*?

- ○ **A.** Firefox
- ○ **B.** Chrome
- ○ **C.** Internet Explorer
- ○ **D.** Safari

6

Which of the following is the native Web browser for Mac OS computers and iOS devices?

- ○ **A.** Firefox
- ○ **B.** Chrome
- ○ **C.** Internet Explorer
- ○ **D.** Safari

7

What is the maximum number of fonts you should include on a single page?

- ○ **A.** 5
- ○ **B.** 2
- ○ **C.** 3
- ○ **D.** 1
- ○ **E.** None of the above

8 You should choose common fonts for your Web pages, because not all fonts are installed on all users' computers.

○ **A.** True
○ **B.** False

9 The two primary characteristics that should be determined for any Web design project are:

○ **A.** Tone and color
○ **B.** Audience and purpose
○ **C.** Purpose and tone
○ **D.** Font and color

10 The logo of a Web site should be placed in the primary real estate, which is located _____.

○ **A.** In the upper right-hand corner
○ **B.** In the lower right-hand corner
○ **C.** In the center of the page
○ **D.** In the lower left-hand corner
○ **E.** None of the above

CHAPTER PROJECTS

These two projects will be used throughout the text. One is a personal project to develop your own Web site geared toward your own career objective. The other is a sample Web site with five pages to allow you to follow the design and development process from start to finish. The sample site is designed to be a creative exercise, so you should be as creative as you can in designing the content for it.

Project 1: Personal Web site

For this project, you will be designing a simple set of Web pages to showcase your experience and skills. When you are finished, you can use this site on business cards and as part of your hiring materials for your career. For the first part of this project, you should write out your purpose and target audience. You should also consider the tone you wish to present and make sure it is consistent with the career path you desire. For example, in a more creative career, you can be less formal and use more color and more whimsical fonts. In your materials for this site, you should decide what information you want to present on this site. Keep in mind that anything posted on the Web is public knowledge, so you should refrain from including information such as a personal phone number or address. Choose an initial color scheme and font set for your site.

Project 2: Creating a Resort Web Site

For this project, you are going to create your own fictional adventure resort. You can choose the location and the types of excursions and services your resort will offer. You should choose five pages for your site, including a homepage and a contact page. The content of the other three pages is your choice. For this part of the project, you should decide on the type of resort, the purpose and audience for your site, and the pages you will include. Choose an initial color scheme and font set for your site. Consider the tone you want to convey with this site.

CHAPTER EXERCISES

1. Choose three travel Web sites (such as *priceline.com* and *travelocity.com*) that offer similar travel options and evaluate which of these sites you believe to have a better design and adherence to purpose. List at least three factors that influenced your decision.

2. Choose three news Web sites (such as *cnn.com*) and evaluate which of these sites you believe to be more credible based only on the design of the Web site. List at least three factors that influenced your decision.

3. Choose three commercial Web sites (such as *amazon.com* and *macys.com*) and evaluate which of these sites you believe to have the best design and adherence to purpose. Explain

which of these sites you would be most likely to use for online purchases. Give reasons for your answer.

4. Visit the Web site of the W3C (*www.w3c.org*). Explain what the intended audience for this site is and what its overall purpose is. Determine whether the design of the site is aligned with your analysis of its audience and purpose. Justify your position.

5. Find an example of a nonprofit Web site in the .org TLD and an example of a commercial Web site in the .com TLD. Explain how the audience and purpose of these two sites differ and explain what they have in common. Justify your position.

6. Find an example of a Web page that is poorly designed. Identify as many as possible of the issues with the design and judge whether they deviate from the intended purpose and audience of the site. Justify your position.

7. Using the template.html file you built in the Activity lessons in the chapter, create a new HTML page called "*myname.html*." Change the title of the page to your name. Add your name to the body of the page. Use the anchor tag to hyperlink your name to your favorite Web site. Save and test your page when you are finished.

8. The <b> tag (which is now deprecated in favor of <strong> but still functions) willbold the text between the <b> and </b> tags. Create a page with text in the body and save it as *bold.html*. Use these tags to bold one of the words in the document. Save and test your page when you are finished.

9. The <i> tag (which is now deprecated in favor of <em> but still functions) will italicize the text between the <i> and

</i> tags. Create a page with text in the body and save it as *italic.html*. Use these tags to italicize one of the words in the document. Save and test your page when you are finished.

10. You can nest HTML tags to add the effects of each tag to the text inside the document. Create a new HTML file and save it as *nest.html*. Add a line of text to the document, wrap the text in the opening tags <b><i>, and end it with the tags </i></b>. The tags should be closed in the reverse order from which they were applied. Save and test your page when you are finished.

CHAPTER REVIEW QUESTIONS

1. Briefly explain the difference between XHTML and HTML. What are the benefits of adhering to XHTML rigor in a Web page? (You may want to use the W3C Web site to help evaluate the differences.)

2. It is important to brand your site consistently. What are the benefits of using a template structure for HTML page creation when you are writing Web pages in a text editor?

3. How would you determine the intended audience for a Web site for a rock band? Briefly explain the factors you would consider.

4. How would you describe the purpose of a news Web site? How would you determine if the site was adhering to its purpose?

5. Find an example of a Web page that uses too many colors in its palette. What is the effect of this on your perception of the Web site? How would you recommend that the site owners correct this issue?

6. When would you recommend using global referencing within a Web site instead of local referencing? What is the benefit of global referencing? What is the benefit of local referencing?

7. Create a sample palette of two primary colors and a secondary color. How do the colors interrelate? Describe why you chose these colors.

8. Suggest a color palette that would accurately represent a Web site dedicated to environmental conservation. Why did you choose these colors, and what do they represent?

9. Readability is one of the key issues to consider when choosing a font for a Web site. On computer screens, sans-serif fonts are easier to read than serif fonts. Describe a type of site that would benefit from using a serif font and what would influence the decision to use it.

10. Why is it important to test your Web pages on multiple browsers? What is the consequence of not testing your pages sufficiently before posting them live on the Web?

Site Planning and Production

This chapter takes a closer look at the planning phase of constructing a Web site. This includes the primary considerations for a site, as well as how to tailor the site to the client's needs. The other important element of this chapter is the introduction to the professional tools for HTML authoring, including Adobe Dreamweaver. You will also learn about how to structure a page based on its expected functionality and the preliminary site modeling. Once you have completed this chapter, you should be able to:

- Describe the process of creating and implementing a Web site through the design and development process

- Direct a client discussion for gathering information to plan a Web site

- Create an initial design set for a Web site based on requirements

- Navigate Adobe Dreamweaver and other professional HTML authoring tools

2.1 WEB SITE PLANNING

If you are designing a Web site or even just a single page for yourself, then you get to choose what you want included, how you want everything to look and feel, and how you want it to flow. However, most often the sites that you create will be either for your organization or for a client. When this is the case, you have to consider the organization's or client's needs above your own preferences and work to deliver the kind of product that meets those needs, tempered with the professional attributes of good site design and flow. This section will introduce you to the overall process of Web site design and construction, techniques for eliciting client requirements, and ways to shape these into an initial design.

2.1.1 The Design and Development Process

There is no single process for designing and developing Web sites perfectly. If you perform an online search for "Web Development Process," you will get a variety of results, with very different terminology and steps. There are, however, two phases to creation of any Web site: design and development. It is possible to spend too much or too little time in either of these processes. The best approach is to move forward steadily in both areas, but you have to establish a starting point in order to do that. Figure 2.1 shows a concise method for Web site construction and represents a repeatable and malleable process that you can adapt to your own needs.

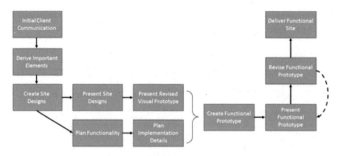

▲ **FIGURE 2.1** The Web Site Design and Development Process

The process outlined in Figure 2.1 will allow you to move forward in both design and development while integrating client feedback. Everything stems from the initial client communication, in which you will ask the right questions to get the client to identify the essential elements of the project. From there, you will distill the responses to your questions to find out what is most important and begin planning the site both visually and functionally. When you have created three initial site designs for the client to review, you will present them as a *design set* to the client for feedback. You should also transition from the planned functionality to a solid plan for implementation, including the languages and server-side resources you will need. Understanding what resources to use will take time and practice, but this text will guide you through planning a few sample projects to get a better idea of what can be accomplished in each language.

After the client has chosen one of the designs, or preferred aspects of the designs, you can create a revised design as a *visual prototype* that you can use to start constructing your site. It is a good idea to get a sign-off from the client on this visual prototype, to make sure it is what he wants in the finished product. By working from this model and integrating some amount of functionality (which may just consist of hyperlinks at this point), you can create a *functional prototype,* on which the final site will be based.

A **prototype** is an initial design or construction representing the finished product in some aspect.

A **visual prototype** (formerly called a paper prototype) is a nonfunctional artistic representation of a Web site, showing how the finished product will look. This prototype is often created in an art program and does not use HTML. This prototype is later discarded.

A **design set** is a series of quick visual prototypes presented to the client. Out of this set, one will be chosen and revised for the client as a final visual prototype to be implemented in HTML code. A **functional prototype** is a working model of a completed Web site in HTML that incorporates some level of the final functionality of the site along with the visual elements of the site design. Once this has been revised and iterated enough, it becomes the final site deliverable.

How often you communicate with the client for each level of implementation will vary depending upon the complexity of the site. If it is a mostly static site presenting information, you may not need more than one or two iterations to complete the site from the initial functional prototype. For more complex and dynamic sites (such as e-commerce sites or business applications), you may want more rounds of presentation and refinement to make sure it is meeting the client's business needs. The back-end construction of the functionality will follow a more traditional software development model than the visual front-end construction, which requires more interaction with the client. Getting the client sign-off on the model and any improvement notes or changes at the end of each presentation will help you keep the project on track and help protect you if there are any problems with the final site implementation. Chapters 3 through 5 of this text focus on the front-end characteristics of the site, and Chapters 7 and 8 focus on the back-end functionality of the site. Chapter 6 presents the JavaScript language (and its common library jQuery), which has applications to both the front end and the back end of the site and can act as an effective bridge between the two pieces of the site itself.

2.1.2 Initial Client Communication

The goals of the initial client communication are to build the client's confidence in what you have to offer and to get a good understanding of what the client expects. If possible, you should try to conduct this meeting in person. This meeting is really not about you and your accomplishments but about the client's vision for the site.

It may be helpful in an initial meeting with a client to come prepared with a repertoire of sites you have constructed in the past loaded for display, because clients like to see that they have chosen someone with demonstrable skill, especially in a market like Web design that is very competitive. If you are new to the field or if you are working on a site for an employer, it is better to omit this and just focus on the client. In fact, you should point out your prior work only if the client specifically requests it.

You need to set a time frame for this meeting, and it should be relatively short. Half an hour should be long enough for the client to convey what he wants from the site if you have the right questions prepared. This is an interview as much as it is a planning session; you need to drive the conversation to the items you need to know in order to proceed with your preliminary design.

One of the additional items you should know before ending the initial meeting with the client is any existing branding the company or client is planning to use on the site. You will have to work within the framework of this branding, such as the color scheme and visual style of what is required on the site. You can ask the client if there is any flexibility on this or just what the required branding will be.

Two key elements you need to understand clearly when you leave this meeting are the audience and the purpose of the site, which are discussed in the next section. You should start by having the client describe for you what his vision of the site is. Try to visualize it from this description and imagine how it might look and feel.

ACTIVITY 2.1 – CREATING A CLIENT QUESTIONNAIRE

For this activity, you should create a list of fifteen to twenty questions that you would ask a client in an initial interview. You should try to keep these focused on the visual aspect of the site and the overall vision of the client. Review your list and determine whether or not any of the questions should be left for later, if any of them pertain to development rather than planning, and whether they can or should be addressed now. Combine or eliminate questions until you have five questions that you feel will adequately capture everything you need to know about the site to start drafting a visual prototype.

Keep the conversation on the issues of branding and visualization. Items like programming languages and implementation details should be saved for later in the process. If you raise these now, you will stall the creativity and cast doubt on your design abilities. If the client wants to talk about technical details, try to give reassurance that those will be handled in the next meeting, but what you really need as a designer at this point is to understand the overall vision.

2.1.3 Establishing Purpose and Audience

This topic was briefly mentioned in the first chapter; it applies to client-driven Web sites as well as to those you design for your own needs. There are two aspects of a site that should guide every decision you make about what goes on every page: the audience and the purpose. The audience of a site is the group of people for whom the site is created. If the site is an entertainment site, the audience will be fans of the group, movie, or whatever is being advertised, and it should address their expectations and needs. If the site is a news site, the audience will be people concerned with the topics on which you are reporting. Determination of the audience should come primarily from the client's intention for the site. If you have enough time during the design phase of the site, you can even interview or survey a sample group to ask what they would want out of a site like the one you are creating. The question to ask about the design elements for this aspect is: do they serve the audience the site is targeting?

Purpose is the other key aspect to consider when planning a site. The purpose of the site is the reason it even exists. The purpose of a Web site may be advertising, information dissemination, information gathering, or any number of other things. The purpose of the site will again come from the client, who should have a clear mission for the site and a reason to construct it.

PROFESSIONAL TIP

The client is often not a Web designer or even familiar with the medium and what it can do. Therefore, you cannot expect them to be completely articulate on their vision of the site or its true purpose without some prompting. You may get answers like, "I was told it has to be constructed in conjunction with Project X." With answers like this, you can delve deeper by asking questions about that project or asking the client why a certain thing is preferable. You should focus on this in conversation until you feel you have elicited the real purpose of the site rather than a superficial answer that will not get you far in constructing the design.

When you are evaluating design choices, you should ask two questions:

1. What is the purpose of this element?

2. How does this element promote the purpose of the site?

If either of the answers is unsatisfactory, then you should consider whether the element should be included in the design. Everything you add to your page should enhance the purpose of the site and serve the needs of the audience. This will become clearer as you begin constructing pages, but keep these principles in mind as you create your visual prototypes. These prototypes will lead directly to the final product, so you should take care in their construction and start asking these questions now.

Nothing undermines confidence in a Web designer/developer like asking clients minute questions about the site whenever an issue arises. If you have a clear audience and a clear purpose, you should be able to answer your own questions by weighing them against these two aspects. If you are contemplating something visual to add to the page, ask yourself a few questions about the site's priorities. **Does this serve the audience of the site? Does it serve the purpose of the site?** These questions will most often give you the answers you need without pestering the client between scheduled meetings.

2.1.4 Emphasizing and Showcasing Content

Part of your task as a designer is to identify what needs to be emphasized on the page. This means establishing visual flow of the page and determining what elements need to receive the most attention. Figure 2.2 gives two layouts using the same visual components but in slightly different ways. Both of these are for a coffee company that is trying to advertise and sell its product to consumers. Which of these two uses the visual emphasis to showcase the product?

▲ FIGURE 2.2 Different Emphases in Visual Design

You want to make sure that the elements important to the audience and purpose receive the most attention on the page. It can be difficult to map where your eye travels and what receives the emphasis. In most Western civilizations, the eye is trained by reading to start at the top left corner of the page and travel to the right and down. You can test your design for emphasis by looking away and then glancing quickly at your design to see where your eye stops on the page first. You should use the visual elements of the page to create a map from the highest-emphasis element to the lowest, which should guide the design of your page (which is part of the branding, which will be discussed later). The eye naturally focuses on the area of highest contrast, so you should make sure that area is where you want your emphasis to be.

2.1.5 Creating a Design Set

When you have an understanding of what the client is expecting, you should begin constructing the design set for the site. The design set is typically three visual prototypes for the Web site. Remember that two of these will be discarded, so you should design them in a low-effort program like Microsoft PowerPoint to produce them efficiently and work more on the layout and what to include rather than the technical aspect of the site. Even if the elements are just mocked up at this point, your job is to convey the overall look and feel of the site in each of the visual prototypes. Each of the designs you create should be unique but should convey the same information. Think of it as three versions of the same exact Web page.) It is helpful to have these printed and ready to share when you meet with the client a second time, so they can be seen side by side and changes can be drawn directly onto a copy of the design.

When you are creating a design set, you should work within the same color palette for each visual prototype. Your client should be deciding between visual nuances in the layout and look of the site rather than choosing between a blue site and a green site.

Creating the design set is one of the most difficult tasks for the front end of a site. You can research similar sites or just review sites that you like and dislike to get an idea of how the page should look. As you progress through the text or your course, you should start to log ten Web sites that work visually and ten Web sites that do not work visually. These will help you to develop a more critical eye for site design and give you a feel for how the user should respond to particular elements in a site.

ACTIVITY 2.2 – WEB SITES THAT WORK AND WEB SITES THAT DON'T WORK

For this activity, you will start a journal of Web sites that work well and Web sites that do not work well. You should confine this to the visual element for now, as you begin to develop a critical eye for designing sites and understanding user interfaces. You should create your journal in Microsoft Word. For each site on your list (good and bad), list the URL and at least three reasons the site either works well or does not work well visually. In Word 2010 or Word 2011, you can insert a screenshot within the document while you have the site open in a Web browser; this will help you later when you revisit your journal.

In all of your site designs, make sure to account for a menu, an area for the menu to expand, and a place for the content to be displayed. The designs you create should not be just a splash or landing page but rather a complete map of what the interior of the site will be once the user gets to the content. You can see an example design set in Figure 2.3.

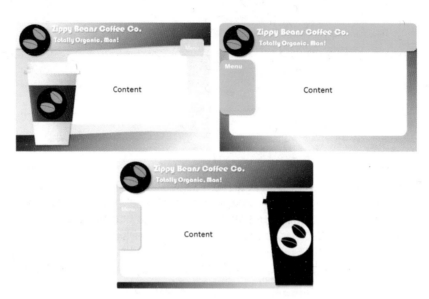

▲ **FIGURE 2.3** Sample Design Set

The splash page (if there will be one) should be designed later, after the content has already been established. You can label these elements on your design for clarity if you do not know what the menu items or content will be at the time you create the design set. Having a clear design and distinct visual elements will help the client understand what to expect in the site.

GUIDING THE DESIGN DECISION

When you present your design set to the client in a second meeting, it is easy to overwhelm them. If the client is not Web savvy and does not have experience with launching Web sites, it is better to help move this process forward by presenting one design that can be eliminated immediately. This should not be a bad design, since you do not want to give a poor impression of your skills, but it should stand apart from the other two as the least interesting. Getting the client to agree to discard this one will give him confidence to move forward in making a decision on the last two designs. This can create a more engaging discussion between you and the client and get you better feedback for refining the final visual prototype that you will create for sign-off after this second meeting.

2.2 THE CASE PROJECT

For the rest of this book, the examples and activities will focus on a fictional coffee company looking to establish a Web presence. Your task is to act as the designer and developer for the functionality they wish to have on their site. The Zippy Beans Coffee Company is a completely organic, high-quality coffee producer with a single store in your town. The palette for the site should be earth tones, greens and browns. The company does have a logo already, but no other branding. You can see the company logo in Figure 2.4.

You can find a copy of this logo in the Web Projects folder of the companion DVD You may also opt to create your own, but using the existing logo will help you learn to establish consistency with existing branding for a Web site. You saw an example of a design set for this case project in Figure 2.3; in Activity 2.3, you will create your own.

▲ **FIGURE 2.4** Logo for Case Project: Zippy Beans Coffee Co.

ACTIVITY 2.3 – CREATING A DESIGN SET

For this activity, you should use Microsoft PowerPoint or an equivalent program to construct a design set for the sample company using the logo the company has already established. (More experienced graphic designers can use Adobe InDesign or Adobe Photoshop, but these should still be throwaway designs.) You should use the earth-tone color palette (greens, browns, and light blues) to construct your design set. Remember that the color scheme should not be a primary distinguishing factor among the different designs.

2.3 PROFESSIONAL HTML AUTHORING TOOLS

While text editors like Notepad are capable of writing HTML code, they are not recommended for professional projects. Instead, you should consider purchasing a professional Web authoring tool. The industry standard for Web development is Adobe Dreamweaver. This is an expensive product; a cheaper alternative is Microsoft Expression Web, which has the same overall functionality. Another tool that you should consider downloading is Notepad++. This is a versatile text editing program that can color-code text for a multitude of different languages, including JavaScript, PERL, and PHP, which will be covered in later chapters. Keep in mind that HTML code is the same regardless of the program that creates it, so you can open the same file in any of the HTML editor programs listed.

You can download a trial version of Adobe Dreamweaver from http://www.adobe.com. You will need to create a free Adobe membership in order to download any of their trial products. If you are a student, you can also get a discounted version of the software from Journey Ed at http://www.journeyed.com.

2.3.1 Adobe Dreamweaver

Adobe Dreamweaver is the industry standard for Web authoring. It is part of the Adobe Master Collection, which includes Adobe Photoshop, the standard for image creation. The Adobe products, particularly Photoshop, have a steep learning curve. However, you can get started with the basic features of the software quickly and learn more as you go. You can see the layout of the interface for Adobe Dreamweaver in Figure 2.5. The figure highlights the key areas you will need to learn so you can use the program to design HTML documents effectively.

The *File* menu and the *Insert* menu are two items in the interface that you will use often to create and manage Web pages. You can use the *File* menu to open files, save files, and create new files. The *Insert* menu is what you will use to add hyperlinks, images, and tables to your HTML document; it has an equivalent panel on the right-hand side of the interface that you can use to visually insert elements into your pages.

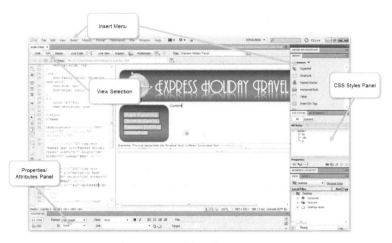

▲ **FIGURE 2.5** Adobe Dreamweaver

The View Selection allows you to choose *Code*, *Design*, or *Split*. The *Code* view shows just the plain HTML text, with color coding to distinguish the tags and text. The *Design* view shows a preview of what the page will look like in a browser. This is called a *What You See Is What You Get* (WYSIWYG) view. The selection *Split* allows you to see the code and the design simultaneously in smaller windows.

ACTIVITY 2.4 – PROFESSIONAL TOOLS

For this activity, you should select and install either the trial or the full version of either Adobe Dreamweaver or Microsoft Expression Web. Create the template page (or open a copy you have already saved) in the program. Describe how the different elements of the page are color coded. How does this improve productivity in scripting HTML?

The Properties (also called "attributes" in HTML) panel is context sensitive. It allows you to adjust the parameters for whatever tag you have currently selected. For an image tag, you can adjust the height and width. For a table, you can adjust the cell padding and border attributes. The CSS Styles panel is where you will manage the integration of CSS commands as you progress farther into the book. There are a multitude of tools and menus available, but this will give you a starting point for exploration and the creation of more dynamic pages.

Microsoft Expression Web

NOTE

You can download a trial version of Microsoft Expression Web from
http://www.microsoft.com/expression. If you are a student,
you can also get a discounted version of the software from Journey Ed at
http://www.journeyed.com.

Microsoft Expression Web is part of the Microsoft Expression suite of programs. It is very similar in layout and functionality to Adobe Dreamweaver, but it costs less. You can see the layout of the interface for Expression Web in Figure 2.6. The figure highlights the key areas you will need to learn so you can use the program to design HTML documents effectively.

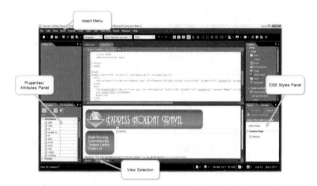

▲ **FIGURE 2.6** Microsoft Expression Web

The interface elements for Microsoft Expression Web are similar to that of Adobe Dreamweaver and both contain similar elements. The *File* menu and the *Insert* menu are the two items in the interface that you will use most often. You can use the *File* menu to open files, save files, and create new files. The *Insert* menu is what you will use to add hyperlinks, images, and tables to your HTML document. The View Selection allows you to choose *Code*, *Design*, or *Both*. The *Code* view shows just the plain HTML text, with color coding to distinguish the tags and text. The *Design* view shows a preview of what the page will look like in a browser. The selection *Both* allows you to see the code and the design simultaneously in smaller windows.

Just like the Properties panel in Dreamweaver, the Attributes panel in Expression Web is context sensitive. It allows you to adjust the parameters for whatever tag you have currently selected. For an image tag, you can adjust the height and width. For a table, you can adjust the cell padding and border attributes. The CSS Styles Panel is where you will manage the integration of CSS commands as you progress farther into the book. There are a multitude of tools and menus available, but this will give you a starting point for exploration and the creation of more dynamic pages.

2.3.3 Notepad++

Notepad++ is available as a free download from **http://notepad-plus-plus.org.** If you use the program and like it, you should consider donating to the organization that produces it. You can do this through the same Web site as the download.

Notepad++ is an excellent tool for programming back-end languages and even front-end languages like JavaScript. It has color coding of elements that shows which pieces of text represent variables, constructs, comments, and strings. You can see an example of the color coding in Notepad++ in Figure 2.7.

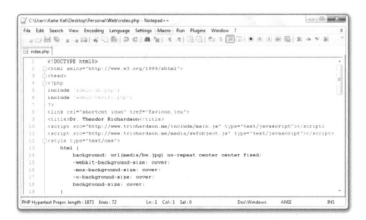

▲ **FIGURE 2.7** Notepad++

As soon as a file is saved through the program, the color coding will be automatically activated for the type of text file it is (such as .html for HTML files and .php for PHP). The color coding will change based on the file type, but coding within an HTML page will register other languages, such as JavaScript. This allows you to see scripts placed within HTML pages as well as the HTML code itself.

CHAPTER SUMMARY

This chapter covered the basic process of designing and developing a Web site. This includes guidelines for communicating with a client and the essential information that needs to be gathered in the initial meeting. Two of the vital pieces of information you must obtain are the audience of the site and the purpose of the site. This will help guide design decisions later in the project and help plan the design set, the alternative designs you offer to your client for review and selection. The outcome of this will be a visual prototype that you will use to construct the final site. The other part of this chapter is the acquisition of the proper tools for developing your site; you should have at least one of these editors and the Notepad++ utility before proceeding to the next chapter. That chapter will cover the translation from your visual prototype to actual HTML code, including image construction and content placement on the page.

CHAPTER KNOWLEDGE CHECK

1 A _____ consists of possible layouts for a Web site from which the client will choose.

- ○ **A.** Visual prototype
- ○ **B.** Functional prototype
- ○ **C.** Design set
- ○ **D.** All of the above
- ○ **E.** None of the above

2 A _____ prototype is one that will be discarded. It should be accurate but quick to construct so not much effort is wasted on its development.

- ○ **A.** Visual
- ○ **B.** Functional
- ○ **C.** Design
- ○ **D.** None of the above

3 A _____ prototype will be iterated repeatedly with improvements until it is handed to the client as a finished product.

○ **A.** Visual

○ **B.** Functional

○ **C.** Design

○ **D.** Throwaway

4 The process for designing and developing a Web site is the same for all organizations and all developers.

○ **A.** True

○ **B.** False

5 Which of the following tools is the industry standard for Web site creation?

○ **A.** Adobe Dreamweaver

○ **B.** Microsoft Expression Web

○ **C.** Notepad++

○ **D.** None of the above

6 Which of the following is one of the essential items a designer must get from the client before developing a design set?

○ **A.** Audience

○ **B.** Purpose

○ **C.** Existing branding

○ **D.** All of the above

○ **E.** None of the above

7 The color scheme of a page should be one of the deciding factors between different designs in a design set.

○ **A.** True

○ **B.** False

8 Color coding in a design tool can help you identify which strings of text are tags and which are content.

   ○ **A.** True

   ○ **B.** False

9 Deciding what content to showcase is the responsibility of the client and not the designer.

   ○ **A.** True

   ○ **B.** False

10 A functional prototype should be shown to the client every time it is updated to a new version.

   ○ **A.** True

   ○ **B.** False

CHAPTER PROJECTS

Project 1: Personal Web site

Using the color scheme you established in Chapter 1, create a design set for your personal site. Remember to allocate enough space in the visual design for content and a menu. Once you have created your design set, review the designs and refine one of them into a visual prototype. Keep all of your designs. You will use your final visual prototype for implementation beginning in the next chapter.

Project 2: Creating a Resort Web Site

Using the design decisions you established in Chapter 1, create a design set for this project. Be sure to allocate space in the visual design for both content and a menu. Once you have created the design set, interview several classmates, co-workers, or family members for their opinions on which design they like most for a vacation location. You should use them as a target audience for choosing and refining your visual prototype. Create the final visual prototype, which will be used for implementing the site beginning in Chapter 3.

CHAPTER EXERCISES

1. Visit three commercial Web sites that advertise products (such as *cocacola.com*). How does each site make you feel about the product? Which of these sites does the best job of showcasing its product? What made you choose this site?

2. Visit three commercial Web sites that advertise services (such as *godaddy.com*). How does each site make you feel about the service? How is the service showcased on the site? Which of these sites does the best job of showcasing its service? What made you choose this site?

3. Use the Internet to research different HTML authoring tools. Select two of these and compare them to Adobe Dreamweaver in terms of functionality, benefits, drawbacks, and cost. Which of the alternatives would you recommend if Dreamweaver were not an option and why?

4. Perform a feature comparison between Adobe Dreamweaver and Microsoft Expression Web. Include items like cost, features, support, languages supported, benefits, and drawbacks in your analysis.

5. What is the purpose and audience for a Web site used as a digital presence for you? How would you target the audience?

6. What is the audience and purpose for a vacation destination site? How would you showcase the destination? You may provide a specific example in your analysis rather than a general strategy.

7. Using the design set you constructed for the case project, explain how you utilized the color scheme and existing branding in your designs.

8. Using the design set you constructed for the case project, explain how you would guide the design decision with the client. Which design would you eliminate first and why? How would you guide the discussion between the remaining two designs?

9. Using the design set you constructed for the case project, explain the transition process you used to get to the final visual prototype. What aspects of the design(s) led to your decision?

10. Describe three ways to showcase the coffee product in the case project without using a coffee cup. Explain the benefits of each of these and select the best alternative. Explain your choice.

CHAPTER REVIEW QUESTIONS

1. Briefly explain why it is important not to spend an enormous amount of time on developing a design set. What are the essential items to include in the design set? Justify your position.

2. Write a strategy for guiding the design decision with a client. What are the main ways to guide the conversation? What are some problems with trying too hard to direct the design decision?

3. Devise a strategy for revising a functional prototype to completion. How often should you show the prototype to the

client? What factors will affect this schedule? What are the drawbacks of showing the prototype to the client too often or not often enough?

4. Why is PowerPoint a good alternative for making a design set? Explain the convenience and drawbacks of using PowerPoint instead of professional image creation software for creating the design sets.

5. Explain why existing branding needs to be a high consideration when planning a Web site for a client.

6. What are the benefits provided by a WYSIWYG view of the HTML code you are constructing for a page? When would this be more useful than just the HTML text? When would the HTML text be more useful?

7. What is the benefit of having color coding in your HTML code view when creating a Web page? How would it help you in designing the page structure? Explain your answer.

8. Why is it important to move technical conversations and considerations to a later discussion with the client after the design set is already in construction? Explain your answer.

9. Why should you arrange to have the planning of the functionality coincide with the creation of the visual prototypes? What benefit does this provide? What difficulties does it create?

10. Why is it essential to derive the correct important elements after an initial client conversation? Consider the scope of the project in your answer (what the project will guarantee at completion).

3

Introduction to HTML

This chapter moves you from the design phase to the development of a functional prototype for your site. Here, you will be concerned with the planning of the site elements over their functionality. As part of this chapter, you will start to create the branding for the site and establish a firm site map so you can plan the navigation correctly. This chapter also introduces you to the basic elements of images and hyperlinks for creating a fully visualized and functional site. Once you have completed this chapter, you should be able to:

- Plan a site layout from a visual prototype

- Construct an HTML layout for a page

- Describe file formats and software for image creation and editing

- Construct images and incorporate them into your HTML document

3.1 CREATING AN INITIAL SITE LAYOUT

Once you have refined the visual prototype for yourself or for a client, you are ready to move into the creation of the functional prototype of the site, which will eventually become the finished product. The planning of functionality on the site is not the primary focus of this book, but you should have a list of functions the site must perform. These functions can range from delivery of static information, such as contact hours and an e-mail address, to complex interaction with a back-end database system that will return dynamic results. The major impact that the desired functionality will have at this stage is on the navigation. However, if you plan your navigation as a section of the page layout with room to expand, then you will likely have no trouble incorporating additional pages (provided you clone your site correctly, which will be discussed later in this chapter). Another area you want to allocate is a consistent area for the main content of each page, where either the static or the dynamic information will be located. This will be a placeholder for the page content; you should have included this in your design set and your revised visual prototype.

3.1.1 Decomposing a Design

In order to properly lay out your page in HTML code, you will need to identify the different sections of the page that you want to include. The easiest way to do this is to draw red lines around the areas in a copy of the visual prototype in whatever program you used to design it. The areas you should mark are:

- Any area where the content changes (for instance, where you may have two objects that overlap on different layers)

- Any area with a distinct purpose (such as a content area or a menu area)

- Any area with a distinct image

- Any area with distinct coloring or shading

- Any area that needs exact spacing (such as a separator image or spacing device)

You should take the time to label each of the sections bordered with red lines. This will help you simplify your coding efforts later. For the labels, you should use names with no spaces, numbers, or special characters; this will allow you to use these names directly in your HTML code to identify the correct section of the design. The exception to this is the background, which will be handled separately. Figure 3.1 shows the final visual prototype for the case project that will be constructed throughout the rest of this text. The lower part of the image shows the notation of the distinct visual areas that you will need to create. This is called decomposing the prototype.

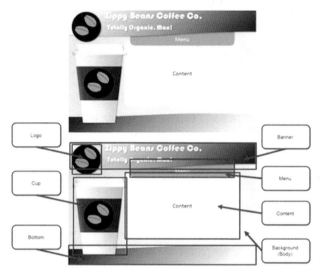

▲ **FIGURE 3.1** Visual Prototype and Section Markup

The majority of the placement and image construction work for the base site will be done in this phase of development. The next few chapters use these same elements and simply refine their placement and positioning. You should always begin your development efforts by structuring the page according to the sections you have created.

ACTIVITY 3.1 – DECOMPOSING YOUR VISUAL PROTOTYPE

For this activity, you will use the final visual prototype you constructed for the case project in Chapter 2. You should use the same program you used to create the visual prototype and create a new copy of it that you will mark with red lines. (You can name it **prototype_markup**.) In the copy, draw lines around every distinct visual area according to the suggested guidelines listed at the beginning of this section. Label each of the sections that you have created by placing these red lines.

3.1.2 Structuring a Page

The default layout for HTML elements is to display each element from the upper left corner going to the right and then moving down the page once the right margin is reached. If you do not use any positioning style commands on your elements, this is the layout with which you are stuck. Fortunately, the next chapter will cover how to change this default behavior. For now, you should concentrate on getting the elements of your site into the page. To begin, you should number each of the sections in the order in which it is initially encountered from the top left to the bottom right; this may not be an exact numbering since there are objects that will overlap. Once again, you should omit the background from this numbering. When you begin coding in the next section, this will be the order in which you enter the elements. You can see an example of this numbering for the sample layout in Figure 3.2.

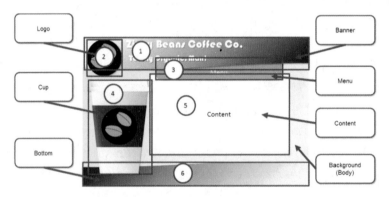

▲ *FIGURE 3.2* Numbered Sections for Sample Layout

3.1.3 Creating Layouts in HTML

If you are just starting out with Web design, you may be tempted to organize your content into a table without borders showing. This was a popular method for constructing layouts prior to the widespread adoption of Cascading Style Sheets (CSS) for positioning. This type of layout is still possible, and for simple, static pages, it can still work. However, the modern approach is to use <div> tags to divide your content into sections and then use CSS to guide the placement of the <div> section. This method will take slightly longer to get to the end product, but it is the professional method. That is the approach that will be adopted for this text. Keep that in mind when you preview your pages in a browser before you get to Chapter 4, when you start to apply CSS.

There is another type of layout called **frames** that was used when Web sites were first becoming popular. These are blocky and cumbersome; in modern Web browsing there is no need for frames, and you should not consider them as an option for any layout.

You should open your template page or create a new template page with the same structure. Create a new project folder called *Zippy*. Save your template page as *index.html* in the Zippy folder. For any site, you should name the first page *index.html*. Every server is programmed to look for this file name in any folder to which it is directed, so you should always make sure that this file is there and that it is the main page of your site. To convert your layout to HTML, you will start by typing the <div> tags into the body of your page.

Each <div> tag should have two attributes within it, an *id* and a *name*. The value used for both of these attributes can be the same. These attributes provide two ways to reference the element, which will come into play later in the text, when you invoke JavaScript to adjust positioning and content. The name and id should both be all lowercase. (They can include numbers as well as letters if there is at least one letter preceding the number.) Between the <div> and </div> tags, you should type the name of the section as a placeholder for content. You should place the <div> tags into your page in the order in which you numbered them in your layout. Remember to exclude the background; that part will be handled separately. For the sample layout, the code for the index.html page should look as follows:

```
<!DOCTYPE html>
<html>
    <head>
    <title>Zippy Beans Coffee Co.</title>
```

```
    </head>
    <body>
      <div id="banner" name="banner">Banner</div>
      <div id="logo" name="logo">Logo</div>
      <div id="menu" name="menu">Menu</div>
      <div id="cup" name="cup">Cup</div>
      <div id="content" name="content">Content</div>
      <div id="bottom" name="bottom">Bottom</div>
    </body>
  </html>
```

The code for the sample layout can be found in the WebProjects folder of the companion DVD in the file layout.html.

As you will see in the coming sections, you can use one file with a completed layout as a template for your entire site. This reduces the overall effort of creating the pages and guarantees that the content on the pages will be displayed the same way from page to page. You can preview your page in a Web browser so you can see how the code positions the <div> elements naturally within the page.

ACTIVITY 3.2 – CREATING A LAYOUT IN HTML

For this activity, you will use the decomposition of your visual prototype for the case project to guide the construction of your index.html file. First, you should create a new project folder called MyZippy. This will distinguish your project from the sample and allow you to develop both of them at the same time. Using the decomposition and coding process outlined for the sample, create your index.html page based on the generic HTML template file. Save your new file as index.html in the MyZippy folder.

3.2 IMAGES

The next step to creating your design is to add images to your page. The available image formats for the Web vary in their characteristics and application, so one of the first tasks is identifying which image format to use in which circumstance. You will also need to consider which elements should be separated into different images. As a general rule, images should be created to be entirely contained within the <div> tag in which they are to be placed without consideration for the background of the image. This section will look at some of the image tools available and how to display images within your page. The <img> tag is the HTML code used to place images within your document.

You may wonder when an image should contain text. In most cases, it is better for the display and better for the overall page to keep text out of images. The exception to this is when the text must be in a particular font that is uncommon to most machines. For instance, the font used for the sample visual prototype for the case project is Bauhaus 93. If this were a real company and that were the font the company used in its logo, it should be included in an image, since this font is not as common as Arial or Times New Roman. If there is a choice of fonts, though, you should opt to type the text in the HTML code and use formatting instead of an image.

3.2.1 Image Formats

There are a number of different file formats for image content. Typical image file formats are JPEG (Joint Photographic Experts Group) File Interchange Format, Graphics Interchange Format (GIF), Bitmap (BMP), Portable Network Graphic (PNG), and Tag Image File Format (TIFF). All of these have specific characteristics and uses, but they are not all suited to the Web. There are two kinds; the primary distinction between them is how the visual information is stored in the file, which determines how much of the information is retained from the original source. These are known as lossless and lossy formats.

Lossless describes a file format that does not lose pixel or color information from the original image source. These tend to be larger files than compressed, lossy formats.

Lossy describes a file format that loses pixel or color information from the original image source. These tend to be compressed and have a smaller file size than lossless formats.

A **palette** is the range of colors that an image file format can contain. Some formats, such as GIF, have a limited palette. Most lossless formats allow a truecolor palette, which contains 16 million colors.

The file formats you should become familiar with for Web design are the following:

- **Bitmap and TIFF**: These are lossless image formats. They tend to have larger file sizes, but they retain all of the image information. Their support for display on the Web is mostly included for older pages of the Web, and these are not recommended as the final format for your images. However, these are great formats to use on a working copy of an image that you are going to convert to a JPG or PNG.

- **GIF**: A GIF image is a limited-palette image that can support 256 colors per image. It is good for images with large areas of the same color but performs poorly for images with gradients and dithering. The GIF format allows image transparency (where part of the image is empty space so the element behind it in the page is visible in that space), and it has an animated version that rotates through a sequence of GIF images using the same color palette. Because of its limitations and the restrictions on creating files in this format, it has largely disappeared from modern Web sites. You should use this format only if you have a specific need for lightweight animation; otherwise you should use the PNG format for transparency.

- **PNG**: The PNG format was created as an open-source successor to the GIF format. The PNG format supports a *truecolor* (16 million colors) palette and allows image transparency. This is an excellent format for layering images, and it is fully supported in modern browsers.

- **JPEG**: The JPEG (or JPG) format is a lossy, compressed format that is well suited to photographs and complex images. This is a well-supported and highly recommended format for images on the Web. The compression method of JPEG files does not work well for images with a large section of the same color; in this case, PNG is the better format to use even though the file size is larger.

Google has developed the WebP (or WEBP) format, which is a lossy compression designed to reduce file sizes for sharing photographs on the Web; so far, JPEG images are still widely used as the standard.

3.2.2 Image Creation Software

The professional standard program for image creation and modification is Adobe Photoshop. This is part of the Adobe Master Collection, along with Adobe Dreamweaver. This is also expensive software, especially if you buy it for commercial use. The learning curve on Photoshop is steep; it has a multitude of tools that you can use to create complex images and perform advanced modification of existing images. You can see an example of a layout for Adobe Photoshop in Figure 3.3.

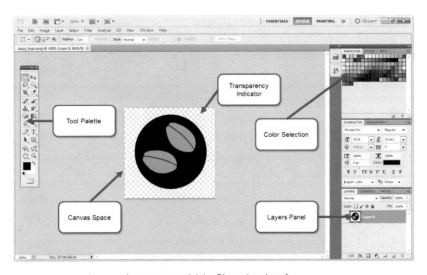

▲ *FIGURE 3.3* Adobe Photoshop Interface

If you are in the business of graphic design and are learning Web design as a supplement to that, it is highly recommended that you obtain a copy of this software. If you are approaching Web design from the programming standpoint and are primarily concerned with the back end of the process, the cheaper alternatives for image creation will most likely suffice.

A free alternative to Adobe Photoshop is the Pixlr® Editor, an online-only software package that provides a substantial subset of the tools available in Photoshop. It can be accessed online at *http://pixlr.com/editor*. This can be used to create transparent PNG images and JPG images. You can see an example of the layout of the Pixlr® Editor interface in Figure 3.4.

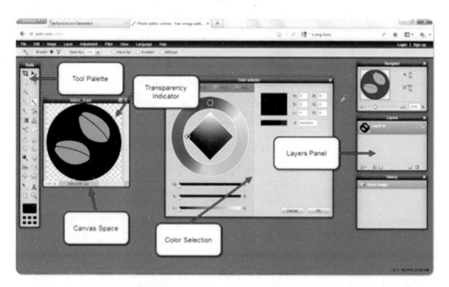

▲ *FIGURE 3.4* Pixlr® Editor Interface from http://pixlr.com/editor

You can even use the Pixlr® Editor to import photos or images from your desktop to edit online. If you are new to image creation, this is a good alternative to Photoshop, since it has a more limited scope of functionality. Additionally, the tools contained in the Pixlr® Editor closely equate to those in Photoshop, meaning that you can learn a tool for Pixlr® and use the same tool in Photoshop with minimal effort.

3.2.3 Creating Site Images

When you are creating images for your site, you should consider the image boundaries and the format you want to use for the image. The primary formats you should use for your images on the Web are JPG and PNG. Photographs and images that do not require transparency and do not have large sections of solid color should use the JPG format. The PNG format is more versatile, but it produces a larger file size than a JPG image. You also need to decide when to use an image and when to use CSS to create the effect.

This is the stage at which you want to spend the time on creation of professional-quality images for your site. These are the images that will go live in the final product.

To evaluate what images need to be created for your site, you can start by going through your layout section by section to decide how to build it in HTML. For the sample layout, the sections can be evaluated as follows:

1. This is the banner section, which will require a background image. Since the image shows the layers beneath it, it will need to be transparent. The image file for this is called *banner.png* within the WebProjects folder of the companion DVD.

2. This is the logo. Since it fits over other layers, it needs to be transparent as well. The image file for this is called *logo.png* within the WebProjects folder of the companion DVD

3. The menu is a solid color. This effect can be achieved using CSS in Chapter 4.

4. This is the cup image. This should be made transparent in order to stack it over the layers beneath it. If this were not transparent, it could fit only in one precise location without disrupting the design. You can see in Figure 3.5 the difference between creating this image for its final placement within the layout (the left image) versus setting it on a background which will become transparent (the right image). The image file for this is called *cup.png* within the WebProjects folder of the companion DVD.

 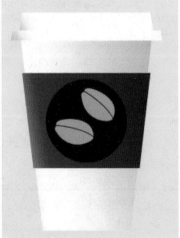

▲ *FIGURE 3.5* Comparison of Backgrounds for Image Placement

5. This is the content area. Once again, this is a solid color. This effect can be achieved with CSS, so no images are necessary.

6. This is the bottom of the interface. Just like the top banner, this layer needs to show the layers beneath it. This will also be used for legal and disclaimer information, so the image created will be used as a background. The image file for this is called *footer.png* within the WebProjects folder of the companion DVD.

To create the effect of the cup image in Pixlr, you can complete the following steps. Create your initial drawing without adding the shadow effect in a photo creation software system (Photoshop, Pixlr, Paint, or even PowerPoint) and save it as a Bitmap file. Open the Pixlr editor in a Web browser and choose the option **Open image from computer**. Select and load your bitmap.

Use the selection tool to highlight the area of the image you want to keep and copy it. Open the File menu and choose **New Image**. In the dialog box that opens, click the checkbox for **Transparent**. (Do not select the **Create image from clipboard** checkbox.) Paste the copied image information into the new image canvas (which should fit perfectly). Use the Wand tool to select the background you want to become transparent and then hit the delete key. If you have done this correctly, you should see a checkerboard background where the image was; this indicates transparency. You can save your image now as a PNG, and it will retain this transparency.

To add a shadow effect like the one used on the cup, go to the layer where your image was pasted and right-click your mouse on the layer image. Select **Layer Styles** from the menu that opens. In the dialog box, choose **Drop Shadow**. You can adjust the parameters of the shadow by clicking on the **Drop Shadow** text within the dialog. Now you can save your image with a shadow that will retain transparency.

Remember that the JPG format is lossy, so you should save your image as a JPG file only one time. You should always have a working copy saved as a PNG, Bitmap, or TIFF. Saving JPG files repeatedly will cause them to lose clarity. You also want to be economical with your file sizes; the larger your file size, the longer it takes to load your page on a client's machine. Too much wasted download time and the client will be off your page before even seeing it. To make sure the file sizes are as small as possible, you should design your images to fit exactly in the space for which they are intended using the sizing features of the image creation tools. This way there is no wasted download time fitting larger files into small spaces when smaller images would serve the same purpose.

ACTIVITY 3.3 — CREATING IMAGES

For this activity, you will create the images needed for your own version of the Zippy Beans site for the case project. Use the analysis of the sample layout to walk through your own design and decide which images need to be created. Create a guide to the images where you analyze what images are needed and record the name of the image you used on a copy of the layout. Save your images in a folder called Media inside your project folder; this will keep your images in one place without cluttering your main folder, which contains the HTML files.

Aside from any additional content you may need later, this is the only image work you will need to do for this project. The Chapter Projects section will ask you to perform the same task for your other projects.

3.2.4 Inserting Images

The tag for inserting images into your HTML document is the <img> tag. This is a self-contained tag that has no closing tag to follow it. Instead, the closing angle (greater than sign) at the end of the tag name is preceded by a space and a slash (<img ... />) to signify that the tag is closed. The important aspect of an image tag is the attributes used to define it:

- *src:* This is the source of the image file. You can use relative addressing or absolute addressing to point to the source file. In relative addressing, you are directing the browser from the location of the current page to the file; for the logo image in a *Media* folder in your project file, you would use src="Media/logo.png" as the src attribute. The absolute address is the complete reference to the image file regardless of where the current page is located. An example of absolute addressing would be src="*http://www.somewhere.com/Media/logo.png*" for the src attribute.

When you are using relative addressing, the character sequence "../" moves up one directory. You can chain these together to move up multiple directories. The character sequence "./" points to the current directory; this is often omitted and assumed (so src="./logo.png" is equivalent to src="logo.png").

- *alt:* The alt attribute contains a text description of the image. This text description is read by browsers for the visually impaired. Including this attribute is imperative for ADA compliance, so it should always be used. It is helpful in any case in which images are disabled in a browser. An example of this would be alt="Zippy Beans Logo" for the *logo.png* file.

- *id:* This is the reference identification for the image within the document. If the image is static and used only for decoration, this can be omitted. However, it is better to include this in the tag in case you need to refer to it in the code. This works as an identifier for the tag and its content the same way it does in the <div> tag.

The <img> accepts other attributes such as height and width, but it is better to use CSS to control these aspects within the design rather than hard coding them in the HTML. For the example layout for the case project, you should create a folder called *Media* in your project folder and move the following files into it: logo.png, banner.png, footer.png, and cup.png.

Some lines of code are longer than the lines of text in this book. Whenever you see a ↵ symbol in the code, the line immediately following it is a continuation that should be on the same line in your actual code. In HTML this is not important but in formal languages it is necessary to keep all of the code on the same line. The code snippets on the companion DVD contain the code in the correct lines for use.

The banner and footer images will be used as background images, so they will not be added until the next chapter. The logo and cup images, however, will be used directly inside the <div> tag for those elements and replace the text you added as a placeholder. The completed code for the added images inside the layout is as follows:

```
<!DOCTYPE html>
<html>
    <head>
    <title>Zippy Beans Coffee Co.</title>
    </head>
    <body>
        <div id="banner" name="banner">Banner</div>
        <div id="logo" name="logo"><img id="logo_img"↵
alt="Zippy Beans Logo" src="Media/logo.png" /></div>
        <div id="menu" name="menu">Menu</div>
        <div id="cup" name="cup"><img id="cup_img" ↵
alt="Zippy Beans Cup" src="Media/cup.png" /></div>
        <div id="content" name="content">Content</div>
        <div id="bottom" name="bottom">Bottom</div>
    </body>
</html>
```

Save your file as index.html in the project folder for the sample site. You can test your code to make sure it works anytime in a Web browser. If you have entered the code correctly and placed your images in the Media folder, you should see two images and the text for the remaining <div> elements.

ACTIVITY 3.4 – ADDING IMAGES TO HTML

For this activity, you should update the HTML page for your version of the case project with image tags. You should add only the tags of the images that are displayed in the foreground of their <div> section. The rest will be added in the next chapter using CSS. You should save your work in index.html and verify that your image links are correct using a Web browser.

CHAPTER SUMMARY

In this chapter, you learned how to decompose a design into sections for implementation in HTML. This included the use and structure of the <div> tag, which is used to segment different pieces of the page, and the order of placement of the sections for display. This chapter also covered the basic use of image creation software and the main formats for image files that can be used on the Web. You learned to analyze which parts of the design need to be turned into images and whether they should be placed in the foreground or in the background. Finally, you learned to use the <img> tag for placing images in your page. The next chapter will show you how to use Cascading Style Sheets (CSS) to format and position the <div> elements and create complex visual styles for your elements with simple commands.

CHAPTER KNOWLEDGE CHECK

1

Which of the following programs cannot be used to create image files?

- ○ **A.** Adobe Photoshop
- ○ **B.** Pixlr Editor
- ○ **C.** Microsoft PowerPoint
- ○ **D.** Microsoft Paint
- ○ **E.** None of the above

2

Which of the following compression types is lossless?

- ○ **A.** Bitmap
- ○ **B.** JPG
- ○ **C.** GIF
- ○ **D.** All of the above
- ○ **E.** None of the above

3

A table layout in HTML will no longer function in a Web browser.

- ○ **A.** True
- ○ **B.** False

4 ____ addressing is the use of the full URL for determining an image location in the src attribute of the <img> tag.

- ○ **A.** Uniform
- ○ **B.** Relative
- ○ **C.** Relational
- ○ **D.** Absolute
- ○ **E.** None of the above

5 Which of the following image file formats supports transparency?

- ○ **A.** JPG
- ○ **B.** Bitmap
- ○ **C.** GIF
- ○ **D.** TIFF

6 Truecolor images define roughly 16 million colors for use.

- ○ **A.** True
- ○ **B.** False

7 An image element should have a transparent background if there is any possibility of its moving on the page based on the size of the browser window.

- ○ **A.** True
- ○ **B.** False

8 GIF images are highly desirable for modern Web sites because of their transparency and ability to show complex animations.

- ○ **A.** True
- ○ **B.** False

9 All image formats are supported by all major browsers, so which file format to use is an individual choice.

- ○ **A.** True
- ○ **B.** False

Once a visual prototype is finalized, the challenge of the Web designer is to make the final HTML site look as close to that design as possible.

○ **A.** True

○ **B.** False

CHAPTER PROJECTS

Project 1: Personal Web Site

For your project in this chapter, you will decompose your visual prototype for your personal site into sections and create the *index. html* page for your project based on the decomposition. You should save this file in the project folder designated for your personal site. Next, you will analyze the sections for which images need to be created, create them, and save them to a *Media* folder within your project folder. Finally, you will add the images into your HTML page using the <img> tag.

Project 2: Creating a Resort Web Site

For your project in this chapter, you will decompose your visual prototype for your resort site into sections and create the *index.html* page for your project based on the decomposition. You should save this file in the project folder designated for your resort site. Next, you will analyze the sections for which images need to be created, create them, and save them to a *Media* folder within your project folder. Finally, you will add the images into your HTML page using the <img> tag.

CHAPTER EXERCISES

1. Choose three Web sites and look at how they layer images within the site. For each site, list the URL and describe the different visual layers used in its layout. Which of these sites creates the most depth? Which of the sites uses images most effectively?

2. A \<div\> tag is a block layout element. Use the Web to research what this means and define it in your own words. What other HTML tags have this default property?

3. Which type of image format is most desirable when download speed is the highest priority on a Web site? What is the tradeoff of using this file type? Justify your position.

4. Create an image as a PNG, a Bitmap, and a JPG. What is the effect of saving the same image repeatedly in each of these formats? Show your results in a Word document with your explanation of the effects.

5. Create a table to compare the features available in Adobe Photoshop with the features of the Pixlr editor. Summarize the key differences and explain why you chose the specific features for comparison.

6. Create a JPG image (from a photo, screen capture, or other source) and convert it to a transparent PNG. Why is JPG a poor format to choose for this type of conversion? What are the artifacts (unwanted pixels) that remain in your image after the transparency is applied? Show your results in a Word document.

7. Look up the reference on the \<img\> tag. What are the available attributes for this tag? Why are only a limited number of them recommended for use in constructing your HTML document? Hint: consider CSS in your answer.

8. One method of decomposing a table layout into \<div\> tags is to add the table to your page using a visual editor (like Adobe Dreamweaver) and adding a \<div\> tag inside of each table cell. Using the sample layout for the case project, explain what the result of this type of table decomposition is. Why is this less effective than creating a <div> layout initially?

9. Another type of tag that divides sections of a page is the <span> tag. Look up the specifications of the <span> tag and compare its use and purpose to those of the <div> tag. Which of these is better for decomposing a visual prototype into sections and why?

10. Give at least three examples in which relative addressing would be less effective than absolute addressing for linking to an image file. Why is absolute addressing not used all the time with images? Justify your answer.

CHAPTER REVIEW QUESTIONS

1. Explain the purpose of decomposing a site into <div> tag sections rather than using a table layout for a design. Are there circumstances in which a table layout would be better to use than a <div> layout? Justify your position.

2. Explain the purpose of choosing an order of elements within a visual prototype. Would this order matter in a table layout? Justify your position.

3. Explain the purpose of placeholder content in establishing a <div> layout. Are there cases when a <div> tag would be completely empty in a display? Justify your answer.

4. Why is it helpful to outline the sections of a visual prototype in red boxes when decomposing a layout? What significance does the rectangle have in these notations, or could any shape be used? Explain your answer.

5. Why should images be created more carefully in the final design rather than using the images from the visual prototype for the final product? Explain your answer.

6. Explain the rationale for always including an alt description of an image in an HTML document, even if the image is purely for decoration.

7. The <img> tag has the functionality to link to a longer description of the image beyond the alt attribute. Give at least two examples of when this would be helpful or even necessary.

8. Why is it important for Web browsers to maintain backward compatibility with older HTML tags and prior layout styles? Justify your position.

9. Explain briefly why construction of HTML pages needs to begin with the visual prototype rather than the functionality of the page.

10. Why is it important to plan all of the elements needed for a page (such as a menu and content area) into the initial visual prototype? What is the consequence of not planning for one of these items?

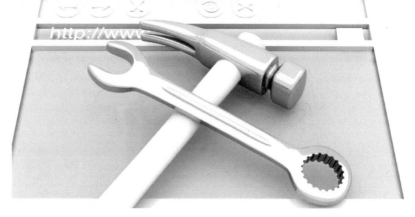

CSS3

The chapter covers the use of Cascading Style Sheets (CSS). The style commands in this language allow you to modify the presentation of your HTML elements in a complex way and achieve unique, layered displays of information and images within a page. CSS commands are essential to site branding and will allow you to create a consistent look and feel across your entire site. Once you have completed this chapter, you should be able to:

- Create a style class

- Use style commands to modify positioning and placement of elements in a page

- Use style commands to modify the color and display of elements in a page

- Create an external CSS document that can be referenced across an entire Web site

4.1 INTRODUCTION TO CASCADING STYLE SHEETS

Cascading Style Sheets (CSS) is a language added to Web design to allow the separation of presentation (or style) from structure. This reduces the amount of code in a page by providing a centralized location for presentation information, which can be reused through tags and classes. CSS3 is the current standard for CSS. A style command works just like an HTML tag attribute. It contains a property and value pair with the structure:

```
property: value(s);
```

You can invoke a style command independently within a tag by using the *style* property. An example of this is:

```
<img src="Media/logo.png" style="width: 150px;" … />
```

In this case, the property is width and the value assigned to it is 150 pixels (px). This is the same as using the code:

```
<img src="Media/logo.png" width="150px" … />
```

The power of style commands is not in their individual use. Instead, their value comes from establishing classes and defining style sets for tags across entire pages and entire Web sites. This section will look at the structure of various CSS classes and their applications. The rest of the chapter will explore some of the specific style commands that are most useful for constructing the layout of your HTML pages. You should keep a copy of your current *index.html* page from the case project (you can save it as *nostyle.html*) as a reference for how much the style commands change the display of the page in a Web browser. Remember that the structure of the page is already established; the style commands simply modify the presentation, or display.

W3Schools (http://w3schools.com) maintains an exhaustive reference for every possible style command. Once you have completed this chapter, you should keep its Web site as a reference for additional style commands and the evolution of new and updated style commands.

4.1.1 Invoking Styles in HTML

In order to use CSS in a Web page, you have to invoke it with a <style> tag. Anything that falls between the <style> and </style>

tags will be interpreted as CSS commands. The <style> tag should be placed inside the <head> tags of a page rather than inside the <body> tags, since it is not defining the actual content to be displayed. The <style> tag has only one attribute, the *type* attribute, which should be set to "text/css" as follows:

```
<style type="text/css">

    ...

</style>
```

You can add comments to the styles using the character string "/*"; this will comment out everything until the character string "*/" is encountered. You can use this to describe the different styles or make notes. You can see an example of this in the following:

```
<style type="text/css">
    /* This is a comment. */
</style>
```

4.1.2 CSS Classes and Tags

The default application of CSS is to apply it to all tags of the same type within an HTML page. For instance, you can set properties for all <div> tags within a page. The structure for this type of style command grouping is as follows:

```
<style type="text/css">
    div {
/* The style property/value pairs go here. */
    }
</style>
```

Anything wrapped within the curly braces ({ and }) will apply to every <div> tag in the page.

If you want your style set to apply only to a subset of tags within the page, you can define a *class* for the style. You define a class by using a period (stop character) before the name of the class (which can be any alphanumeric character string as long as it starts with a letter).

For instance, you can define a *logo* class using the following:

```
<style type="text/css">
    div {
/* The style property/value pairs go here. */
    }
    .logo {
        width: 150px;
}
</style>
```

You can define multiple style sets and classes within the same set of <style> tags. To invoke a class, you must call it within the tag to which you want the style set to apply. To call the *logo* class, you would use the following:

```
<img src="Media/logo.png" class="logo" … />
```

When calling a style class, you do not need the period before the class name. This is necessary only when you define the class itself.

4.1.3 CSS IDs

Style sets can also be defined for an individual element within a page. The problem with doing this is that the style set is used only once and cannot be invoked again later. The benefit of doing this is that you do not need to invoke the class call for the style to apply. In cases where the HTML is dynamically generated or changed during display, this can be an easier way to apply styles than with class calls. To define a style for a particular element, you just need to know the element's *id* value. To apply a style to a specific tag based on its *id* value, you define the style set using a hash symbol (#). You can see an example of this type of style definition in the following:

```
<style type="text/css">
    #logo {
```

```
            width: 150px;
    }
</style>
```

In this example, the style set defined would apply only to the element with the attribute *id="logo"* within the page. The element id must be unique for the page to work properly. There is no need to invoke the style; it will be applied automatically.

4.1.4 Pseudo-classes

Another type of class within CSS is a *pseudo-class*. This type of class is invoked depending on the *state* of the tag to which it is applied. One of the most common applications of a pseudo-class is with hyperlinks, which you will see in Chapter 5. When a user hovers the mouse over the hyperlink, the tag enters the state *hover*; you can use this state to define a pseudo-class that will change the style properties only while this state is active. The "hover" state would become inactive when the mouse leaves the hyperlink element and the style set in the pseudo-class would no longer apply. You can apply this pseudo-class to other elements as well, particularly <div> tags.

The pseudo-class is a subclass of a tag, a class, or a tag *id*. You define a *hover* pseudo-class for the *logo* class using the following code:

```
<style type="text/css">
    .logo:hover {
            width: 180px;
    }
</style>
```

Now when a user hovers over the tag invoking the *logo* class, the width of the tag will change to 180 pixels.

There are a number of available pseudo-classes, including *hover, visited, active,* and *focus.* As you learn more about hyperlinks, you may want to revisit this topic to determine how to tailor your link display based on current or prior user actions. You will use the *hover* pseudo-class to expand the menu in the sample layout in this chapter.

4.1.5 Inheritance

CSS is designed to allow elements to *inherit* styles from their parent tags (the tags that contain them). The simplest example of this is that any text modifications defined for the <body> tag will apply to all tags and elements within the <body> tag. This inheritance also allows you to define certain styles once and then ignore that property later. For instance, if you set the font for the <body> tag, you do not need to set the font again unless you want a different font within a specific set of tags or element.

In some browsers, <table> tags do not inherit from the <body> tag. This is also true for form elements. You can force properties to be inherited by setting their value to inherit in the style definitions for the tags that are not cooperating. This prevents you from having to define the same code multiple times, because it will force changes in the <body> tag to apply to any tag whose value specifies that it should inherit that property value.

The style commands that are closest to the actual element are applied first for that element. This means that any style commands for an invoked class will supersede style commands for the tag, which will supersede style commands for the parent element. These inheritance rules can be applied in interesting ways. An element can inherit styles from a parent, a class, a tag, and an ID. You can also invoke multiple classes in CSS and define classes for nested elements, but this can be overwhelming when you are first getting started.

4.2 POSITIONING AND LAYERING

When you render a page in HTML, the default positioning for any element is to be placed as it appears in the document, one element after another. This is called static positioning. For simple layouts this may suffice. For a long time, this was the only option for positioning elements. With CSS, however, you have the ability to position elements wherever you want them on the page. This is accomplished using the *position* property in a style command. In order to actually move the element around within the page or within the browser window, you need to use several other properties to establish where the element should appear. These additional properties set any or all of the following: the left and top displacement, the layering, the height and width, and the margins and padding for an element. These properties give you precise control over your layout and over how each element appears within the browser window.

4.2.1 Element Position

The *position* property controls how the element positioning is handled within the page display. In order to make adjustments to the element, you must first know how it will be positioned within the page. There are several possible *position* values to consider for an element:

- *Static:* The items are positioned on the page in the order in which they appear in the HTML document. This is the default case.

- *Inherit:* The positioning of the element is based on the *position* property value of the parent. You can commonly set more property values to *inherit* to force them to take on the parent characteristic for that property.

- *Absolute:* This positions the element in relation to its first positioned parent (which is most often the <body> tag). This is the most common positioning you will use for elements that you still want to scroll on the page but also want to retain their position on the page.

- *Relative:* This positions the element at an offset from its parent element. For instance, you can set a left value of 20 pixels, which will place this element 20 pixels to the right of the parent.

- *Fixed:* This setting positions the element relative to the browser window itself. It will fix the item in place and will not allow it to scroll on the page. This is useful for banner and menu items that you want to have always appearing on your page regardless of the length of the content.

An example of the *position* property can be seen in the following:

```
<style type="text/css">
    #banner {
        position: fixed;
```

```
        }
    </style>
```

Setting this value does not by itself alter the appearance of the element at all. In order to do this, you must set an *anchor point* for the element on the page. For this, you will typically use the *top* and *left* properties (though combinations of the *top, bottom, left,* and *right* elements can be used to define an anchor point at any of the corners of the element).

In CSS, the abbreviation **px** following a number represents the number of individual pixels the **property** value should be, so 100px is 100 pixels. The number of pixels in the display area is governed by the display resolution of the viewer's monitor.

The following is an example of this that will place the *banner* element in the sample case project layout at the top left corner of the browser window:

```
<style type="text/css">
    #banner {
            position: fixed;
            top: 0px;
            left: 0px;
    }
</style>
```

If you cannot see the effect of this, you can make your browser window smaller until there is enough content to allow you to scroll the page.

An **anchor point** consists of the vertical and horizontal coordinates of a single point that define how an element is placed on a page. The anchor point is typically the top left corner of the element, but it can be defined at any point within the element, depending on the application.

The next step in your layout construction is to set the positioning and the anchor points for the <div> tags in your page. For the sample layout for the case project, each of the <div> tags should be analyzed for placement:

- **Banner:** The banner should be placed in a fixed position so it always appears above the content itself. It should start at the upper left corner of the browser.

- **Logo:** The logo should appear on top of the banner element, so it should also be fixed. It should appear at the upper left of the browser, but some padding will be added to it later.

- **Menu:** This should be fixed beneath the banner so it is always on display but hidden under the branding of the banner. This will be offset into the page so it rests on top of the content.

- **Cup:** This element is for display only; it is the image of the coffee cup shown in the sample layout. Its location can be fixed to establish consistency even if the content scrolls. It should be placed behind the banner and logo and offset lower into the page.

- **Content:** This should be an expandable area where the main content of each page will be displayed. It should have an offset so it begins behind and to the right of the cup. The width of this element will be fixed so that it can grow as needed only in the vertical direction.

- **Bottom:** This is the end of the branding. This section will contain the disclaimer, which can be hidden from view off the screen as long as it is on the page. It can be either fixed, so the content is viewed as a scrolling window within the branding, or allowed to move with the page. The choice on this is left to you; for the sample, it will be fixed at the bottom to show you how this can be done.

In CSS, this translates to the following style sets for the sample layout:

```
<style type="text/css">
    #banner {
        position: fixed;
        top: 0px;
```

```
            left: 0px;
      }
      #logo {
            position: fixed;
            top: 0px;
            left: 0px;
      }
      #menu {
            position: fixed;
            top: 80px;
            left: 220px;
      }
      #cup {
            position: fixed;
            top: 160px;
            left: 0px;
      }
      #content {
            position: absolute;
            top: 140px;
            left: 200px;
      }
      #bottom {
            position: fixed;
            bottom: 0px;
            left: 0px;
      }
</style>
```

Note the positioning of the *bottom* element. You can use percentages as well as exact pixel numbers for values. By setting this *bottom* property value to 0, you keep it at the bottom of the page no matter what size the browser window is. The value of the *bottom* property is the distance above the bottom of the containing element, which in this case is the <body> tag. If you test this page in a browser, you will start to see the layout coming together, but as you expand the CSS style set for each element, your design will come closer and closer to the visual prototype you designed!

ACTIVITY 4.1 – CREATING STYLE SETS

For this activity, you will analyze your visual prototype for the case project and decide on the positioning for each of the elements on the page (each section that you defined with a <div> tag). Using the <style> tag, create the initial style sets for the element IDs (using a # prefix). As you plan this out, consider the height and width you want to use for each element in your design. Keep in mind the expected layout size in pixels that you will use as you plan these elements. Chapter 1 has the standard layout guidelines for modern browser and display sizes.

4.2.2 Layers

Even after the positioning of the elements is set, two elements cannot reside in the same space on the same layer. The CSS property that governs the layer used is the *z-index* property. The value of this property is a number representing the stack order from background to foreground. The lowest number is furthest in the browser background, and the highest number is closest in the foreground.

The depth distance (along the z-axis) between elements is not determined by the relative values of the z-index property. A difference between 1 and 2 in property values for two elements has no display effect compared to property values between 1 and 500 for two elements.

In order to set the stack order with *z-index* values, you need to consider which element should be on the bottom of the stack and work your way forward. A best practice is to set your <body> tag at *z-index* value 1 and build forward. For your convenience, you can increment the *z-index* values by 5 or 10 to allow the addition of other elements in a redesign later. With the analysis in the prior section on the <div> elements in the page, the following is the updated style set:

```
<style type="text/css">
    #banner {
            position: fixed;
            top: 0px;
            left: 0px;
            z-index: 30;
    }
    #logo {
            position: fixed;
            top: 0px;
            left: 0px;
            z-index: 40;
    }
    #menu {
            position: fixed;
            top: 80px;
            left: 220px;
            z-index: 20;
    }
    #cup {
            position: fixed;
            top: 160px;
            left: 0px;
            z-index: 10;
    }
    #content {
            position: absolute;
            top: 140px;
            left: 200px;
    }
```

```
#bottom {
        position: fixed;
        bottom: 0px;
        left: 0px;
        z-index: 30;
    }
</style>
```

4.2.3 Height and Width

In addition to positioning, it is a good idea to set the height, the width, or both for an element. The *height* and *width* CSS properties can be set for any element. You can specify a value in pixels (px), percentages (%), or elastic measurements (em). If both of these properties are set for an element, they can be set in different base units.

An **elastic measurement** is a multiplier on the base font size of the parent element. For most browsers, this is a default 16px, but it can be changed by the user for readability, and it allows the design to be scaled with the text. An elastic value of 0.75em on a default element would be 0.75 · 16px = 12px as an actual pixel measurement. This can take some practice, but with time it can be as precise as a pixel-based layout.

For this part of the layout refinement, you should consider which elements have to span the entire page, which elements should have a fixed size, and which elements should be allowed to grow. In the example below, the banner and footer should span the entire width of the page. The content area should be allowed to grow vertically (but should have a fixed width). The images should be fixed in size in both directions.

In addition to the <div> tags, you can use the *height* and *width* properties to set the parameters for the images themselves within the page. If these properties are left blank, the default behavior of the <img> tag is to display the image at 100% of its height and width according to the file size of the image. The height and width decisions for the sample layout for the case project result in an update to the

CSS style sets (and the inclusion of new style sets to define sizing):

```
<style type="text/css">
    #banner {
            position: fixed;
            top: 0px;
            left: 0px;
            z-index: 30;
            width: 100%;
            height: 150px;
    }
    #logo {
            position: fixed;
            top: 0px;
            left: 0px;
            z-index: 40;
            height: 175px;
            width: 175px;
    }
    #logo_img {
            height: 150px;
            width: 150px;
    }
    #logo_img:hover {
            height: 175px;
            width: 175px;
    }
    #menu {
            position: fixed;
            top: 140px;
            left: 220px;
            z-index: 20;
            width: 760px;
    }
    #cup {
```

```css
            position: fixed;
            top: 160px;
            left: 0px;
            z-index: 10;
    }
    #cup_img {
            width: 220px;
            height: 306px;
    }
    #content {
            position: absolute;
            top: 160px;
            left: 200px;
            width: 800px;
    }
    #bottom {
            position: fixed;
            bottom: 0px;
            left: 0px;
            z-index: 30;
            width: 100%;
            height: 116px;
    }
</style>
```

When you are testing your layout as it develops, you can add a temporary class to the <div> tag so you can see where the element sits on the page. The class you should add is:

```css
div {
    border-style: solid;
    border-width: 5px;
    border-color: red;
}
```

The example above includes CSS code for the *hover* pseudo-class on the *logo* image; this will increase the size of the image whenever the user hovers the mouse over it. This will be useful when the link to the home page is added to this image. Any kind of effects like this that you can add with CSS will maintain cross-compatibility and eliminate the need for JavaScript coding, which tends to be more browser-specific and complex.

 You can check the height and width of an image by clicking on the file in Windows Explorer in Windows 7. If these values are not automatically displayed or if you are using a different OS that does not include this functionality, you can right-click and select Properties to get this information.

4.2.4 Margins and Padding

There are two property sets that help define both positioning of the element itself and placement of content within the element. The *margins* define how far the element resides from its neighboring elements or from the border of the browser. The *padding* defines how far inside the surrounding element the content starts. You can define the padding or margins for each of the sides: *top, bottom, right,* and *left.* You can see an example of these properties in the following:

```
div {
    margin-top: 20px;
    padding-left: 20px;

}
```

You can see the added padding and margins for the sample case project layout in the following code:

```
<style type="text/css">
    body {
            margin-left: 0px;
            margin-right: 0px;
            margin-top: 0px;
            margin-bottom: 0px;
    }

    #banner {
            position: fixed;
            top: 0px;
            left: 0px;
            z-index: 30;
            width: 100%;
            height: 130px;
            padding-left: 200px;
            padding-top: 10px;
            padding-right: 10px;
    }
    #logo {
            position: fixed;
            top: 0px;
            left: 0px;
            z-index: 40;
            height: 175px;
            width: 175px;
            margin-left: 20px;
    }
    #logo_img {
            height: 150px;
            width: 150px;
    }
```

```css
#logo_img:hover {
      height: 175px;
      width: 175px;
}
#menu {
      position: fixed;
      top: 80px;
      left: 220px;
      z-index: 20;
      width: 780px;
      height: 60px;
      padding-top: 20px;
}
#cup {
      position: fixed;
      top: 160px;
      left: 0px;
      z-index: 10;
}
#cup_img {
      width: 220px;
      height: 306px;
}
#content {
      position: absolute;
      top: 140px;
      left: 200px;
      width: 800px;
      padding-left: 20px;
      padding-right: 20px;
      padding-top: 35px;
      padding-bottom: 20px;    }
#bottom {
```

```
            position: fixed;
            bottom: 0px;
            left: 0px;
            z-index: 30;
            width: 100%;
            height: 80px;
            padding-left: 10px;
            padding-right: 10px;
            padding-top: 0px;
        }
    </style>
```

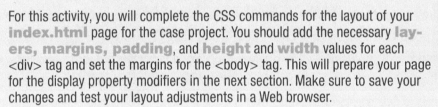

4.3 DISPLAY PROPERTIES

CSS is a powerful tool not just for positioning and element placement but for altering the display of the elements as well. This behavior was previously reserved for a <font> tag, which is now unnecessary (and deprecated). Part of the display-oriented CSS is control of the background, coloring, borders, shadows, and font selection. These properties can be applied to classes, tags, and element *id* values.

4.3.1 Background Images

Using CSS, you can add a background image to a tag. This works well for block-display elements like <div> tags. The property to use for this is *background-image,* and its value should be either the relative or the absolute path to the image from the current page (even if the

CSS is located externally, as you will learn in the last part of this chapter). In order for this to be used in CSS, you need to wrap the path in a function to convert the text to a URL with *url('./string value')*. An example of this is:

```
#banner {

    ...

background-image:url('./Media/banner.png');
}
```

There are a number of additional support properties that can modify the placement and attachment of the background image to the tag. One of the key properties is *background-size,* which sets the width and height of the background image for the tag (as two separate values). The property *background-repeat* determines whether the image will tile in one or both directions (or neither); the available values for this are *repeat* (which tiles in both directions), *repeat-x* (which tiles horizontally), *repeat-y* (which tiles vertically), and *no-repeat* (which uses the image only once). The property *background-attachment* can be set to *scroll* (which allows the image to scroll with the content) or to *fixed* (which keeps the background in place). The *background-position* property sets the relative position of the image. The available values for this can be any of the set *{left, right, center}* combined with any of the set *{top, bottom, center}* or can be a horizontal value (percentage or measurement offset) and a vertical value (percentage or measurement offset).

These properties can be combined and used as needed. For the sample layout, the following are used to set the background images for the banner and the footer of the page:

```
<style type="text/css">

    ...

#banner {

        ...

        background-image:url('./Media/banner.png');
        background-repeat:no-repeat;
```

```
            background-position: top;
            background-size: 100% 130px;
        }
        ...

        #bottom {
            ...
            background-image:url('./Media/footer.png');
            background-repeat:no-repeat;
            background-size: 100% 80px;
            background-position: bottom;
        }
    </style>
```

4.3.2 Colors

You can use CSS to define colors for use in backgrounds as well as colors for the content (mostly the text that displays in an element). The two properties for color are *background-color* and *color*. The *background-color* property is used to define the color behind the content; this can be used in conjunction with a transparent background image in most browsers, as long as the color is defined before the background image. The *color* property is used to define the text and content foreground color. You can see an example of this in the code:

```
#menu {
    ...
    background-color: #3c3;
    color: #efe;
}
```

There are a variety of values that can be used for color in either of these properties. There are named colors that can be used, such as *red, green,* and *blue.* There are 17 base colors, which are recognized across all browsers as standard. You can see a list of all standard colors at the W3Schools site: *http://www.w3schools.com/cssref/css_colornames.asp.* You can also specify individual color values in one of two formats:

- *Hexadecimal (hex):* These values use a # mark to signify the start of the code and use a *#RedGreenBlue* or *#RGB* format, such as *#0f0* for pure green. A more specialized form of this uses two hexadecimal characters for each color instead of one. This format allows you to specialize the color even more; an example of this is *#a347a3* for a specific shade of purple. The three-character version of a hexadecimal code is shorthand for both characters allocated for a single color being the same. Each color in hexadecimal notation has a range of intensity from 0 to 255 (or *ff*).

- *Red Green Blue Alpha (RGBA):* In this alternative format for displaying color, the color values are represented in standard integer values ranging from 0 to 255. The alpha value is used to determine the transparency and ranges in decimal values from 0 to 1, where 0 is completely transparent and 1 is fully opaque. An example of this is *rgba(0,255,0,1)* for pure green with full opacity. You can specify percentages for the color values instead of integers (up to 100%). An alternative form of this format omits the alpha value, as in *rgb(0,255,0)* for pure green.

The W3Schools site maintains a color picker tool for choosing any color and getting its hexadecimal representation. The address for this tool is http://www.w3schools.com/tags/ref_colorpicker.asp.

A more complex application of the color properties can be used to create a gradient effect as the background of a content area on the page. A great tool for creating this can be found at Damian Galarza's page at *http://gradients.glrzad.com*. The code for this is very browser-specific, so you have to include multiple CSS style commands in the *style* set; the other codes that are not part of the browser just get ignored. The tool will generate the code for all browsers that accept gradients. This will be used for the gradient background in the sample layout design (which will be attached to the <body> tag). For this to work, you should have a width and height specified as well as background attachment and repeat properties. You should also choose a single background color for browsers in which the gradient CSS is not supported. The gradient code generated by the tool described is as follows:

```
body {
    …
    height: 100%;
    width: 100%;
    background-color: #E0FFD1;
    background-attachment: fixed;
    background-repeat: no-repeat;
    /* The gradient information follows. */
    background-image: linear-gradient(left top, ↵
#4BE60E 2%, #E0FFD1 65%);
    background-image: -o-linear-gradient(left top, ↵
#4BE60E 2%, #E0FFD1 65%);
    background-image: -moz-linear-gradient(left top, ↵
#4BE60E 2%, #E0FFD1 65%);
    background-image: -webkit-linear-gradient ↵
(left top, #4BE60E 2%, #E0FFD1 65%);
    background-image: -ms-linear-gradient(left top, ↵
#4BE60E 2%, #E0FFD1 65%);
    background-image: -webkit-gradient(
                       linear,
                       left top,
                       right bottom,
                       color-stop(0.02, #4BE60E),
                       color-stop(0.65, #E0FFD1)
    );
    /* This is the end of the gradient information.
*/
}
```

The CSS color codes for the different design elements in the sample design layouts are as follows:

```
<style type="text/css">
```

```
body {
        height: 100%;
        width: 100%;
        background-color: #E0FFD1;
        background-attachment: fixed;
        background-repeat: no-repeat;
        background-image: linear-gradient(left top, ↵
#4BE60E 2%, #E0FFD1 65%);
        background-image: -o-linear-gradient(left ↵
top, #4BE60E 2%, #E0FFD1 65%);
        background-image: -moz-linear-gradient(left ↵
top, #4BE60E 2%, #E0FFD1 65%);
        background-image: -webkit-linear-gradient ↵
(left top, #4BE60E 2%, #E0FFD1 65%);
        background-image: -ms-linear-gradient(left ↵
top, #4BE60E 2%, #E0FFD1 65%);
        background-image: -webkit-gradient(
                linear,
                left top,
                right bottom,
                color-stop(0.02, #4BE60E),
                color-stop(0.65, #E0FFD1)
        );
    }
...
    #banner {
        ...
        color: #fff;
    }
...
    #menu {
        ...
        background-color: #3c3;
        color: #efe;
```

```
        }
        ...

    #content {

            ...
            color: #010;
            background-color: #fff;
    }
    #bottom {

            ...
            background-position: bottom;
            color: #fff;
    }
    ...

</style>
```

4.3.3 Borders

CSS allows you to set borders for your elements as well. You can do this with the *border-width, border-style, border-color,* and *border-radius* properties. The last of these can be used to establish custom radii for each corner of the tag boundary. All of them are best used in combination with the *background-color* or *background-image* property. These properties take specific values:

- *Border-width:* This property uses either a percentage or a measurement.

- *Border-style:* This uses a specific value, such as *groove, solid, dashed,* or *double*; a complete list of these can be found at *http://www.w3schools.com/cssref/pr_border-style.asp.*

- *Border-color:* This accepts the color formats discussed in the previous section.

- *Border-radius:* This property accepts either a percentage or a measurement.

The *border-radius* property has modifiers, which can specify the corner to be changed. For example, the menu needs only rounded bottom left and bottom right corners. The properties for this are *border-bottom-left-radius* and *border-bottom-right-radius.* You can see the code for rounding the menu and content <div> tags for the example in the following code:

```
<style type="text/css">
    ...
#menu {
        ...
        border-bottom-left-radius: 16px;
        border-bottom-right-radius: 16px;
}
    ...
#content {
        ...
        border-radius: 16px;
}
</style>
```

4.3.4 Shadows

Another useful property in CSS is the *box-shadow* property. This allows you to add shadows to layered content, which can add a sense of depth and perspective to the layout of your page. The *box-shadow* property is supported in most of the main modern browsers, but Safari supports the *-webkit-box-shadow* property, which you should include as a separate line in the CSS style set. The parameters (in this case a set of values) for *box-shadow* are as follows:

- *H-shadow:* This is the horizontal distance by which the shadow should be offset; this value is required.

- *V-shadow:* This is the vertical distance by which the shadow should be offset; this value is required.

- *Blur:* This is the distance over which the shadow should be blurred; this value is optional and defaults to 0.

- *Spread:* This is the distance over which the shadow should spread; this value is optional and defaults to 0.

- *Color:* This is the color of the shadow; this value is optional and defaults to pure black.

- *Inset:* This value sets the shadow to be internal; to enable this, just add the text *inset* to the end of the parameter list.

In the sample layout, this is added to the *menu* element of the design. You can see the code for this in the following:

```
<style type="text/css">

    ...

#menu {

        ...

        box-shadow: 2px 2px 6px 0px #030;
        -webkit-box-shadow: 2px 2px 6px 0px #030;

}

    ...

</style>
```

4.3.5 Content Alignment

You can use CSS to align content within a tag both vertically and horizontally. The *text-align* property is used to align the content *left, right, center,* or *justify.* (Each line has equal width.) The *vertical-align* property is used to vertically orient the content within a tag; the common values for this property are *top, middle,* and *bottom,* though others exist. The issue with vertical-align is that it applies only to table cells (or elements formatted with *display: table-cell* in more advanced CSS). You can see an example of the content alignment for the logo <div> tag that contains the image in the following code:

```
<style type="text/css">

    ...

    #logo {

        ...

        text-align: center;

}

    ...

</style>
```

4.3.6 Text Modification

There are a number of different properties that control the display of text within an element. These are some of the simpler CSS commands to use, and most of them have been around since CSS version 1. The common text adjustment properties, their descriptions, and their accepted values are as follows:

- *Font-family:* This property defines the order in which the browser will seek fonts to render the contents of the tag. The value for this is a comma-separated list of font names. It is a good idea to end the list with either *serif* or *sans-serif,* which are the default fonts for these categories in case no other font in the list can be found. If there are spaces in the font name, you have to add single quotation marks around the name of the font or it will not read as a single font. An example of this is *font-family: Arial, Helvetica, sans-serif;*

- *Font-size:* This defines the size of the font. (Remember that a font is both a typeface and a size.) The value of this property is a measurement, which can include traditional point (pt) values for font size in addition to the other measurements discussed for placement. An example of this is *font-size: 10pt;*

- *Font-weight:* This describes whether text is normal or modified to be lighter or bolder. The common values for this are *normal* (default) and *bold* (bold type). An example of this is *font-weight: bold;*

- *Font-style:* This property is used to italicize text. The common values for this are *normal* (default) and *italic*. An example of this is *font-style: italic;*

- *Text-decoration:* This property is used to apply text decorations such as strikethrough and underline. The common values for this are *none* (default except for hyperlinks) and *underline*. An example of this is *text-decoration: none;* (which actually removes the underline from a hyperlink).

- *Text-shadow:* This is a unique property that allows you to add a shadow to the text in an element. This property takes a series of values: *h-shadow, v-shadow, blur,* and *color.* The values *h-shadow* and *v-shadow* are required; they are the offset distances in, respectively, the horizontal and the vertical distance from the text. The values *blur* and *color* are optional. The *blur* value is the distance over which the shadow blurs, and the *color* value accepts color input and determines the base color of the shadow. An example of this is *text-shadow: 2px 2px 3px #010;*

You can see the text modifiers added to the *style* sets for the sample layout for the case project in the following code:

```
<style type="text/css">
    body {
            ...
            font-family: arial, helvetica, sans-serif;
            font-size: 12pt;
    }
    #banner {
            ...
            font-family: 'Bauhaus 93';
            font-size: 36pt;
            text-shadow: 2pt 2pt 4pt #020;
    }
    ...
    #menu {
            ...
            font-size: 10pt;
    }
    ...
    #content {
            ...
            text-shadow: 1px 1px 2px rgba(0,10,0,0.2);;
    }
    ...
</style>
```

ACTIVITY 4.3 – MODIFYING ELEMENT DISPLAY WITH CSS

For this activity, you will incorporate the display adjustment properties of CSS into your evolving style sheet for the index.html page of your case project. You should not define new HTML elements to adjust your display at this time; instead, you should focus on establishing the effects for your layout of using CSS on the existing HTML tags and IDs, including the <body> tag. You can test the results in a Web browser to be sure you have done this correctly. Feel free to modify the CSS as needed until your page is displayed correctly. You should test your result in at least two of the major browsers: Internet Explorer, Mozilla Firefox, Apple Safari, and/or Google Chrome.

4.4 REUSING CSS STYLES

Now that you have a better understanding of how to use CSS to format the display of elements, you should learn to reuse your CSS across your entire Web site. This will allow you to further capitalize on the power of CSS by defining the styles in one central location to apply to all pages. As your site grows, this becomes more important. Imagine if you had to change one property for a particular style that was redefined in every page of a fifty-page site? With an external style sheet, you would need to change only one value in one location.

To create an external style sheet, you should first create a new subfolder within your project folder called *Include*. Create a new file in a text editor like Notepad++ and save it as *styles.css* within the *Include* folder. Copy the styles you have defined in your *index.html* page (everything between the <style> and </style> tags) and paste it into this new text document. The file extension *.css* tells the browser what kind of content the file contains.

To invoke this file, you need to use a <link> tag to connect to an external resource. The link tag has several properties:

- *rel:* This defines the relationship (how the resource interacts) between the current document and the referenced document. In this case, it is *stylesheet*.

- *Type:* This defines the type of content the browser should expect. For CSS, this is *text/css.*

- *href:* This stands for hyper-reference; it is the location of the document in relation to the current page on the server. This is used the same way the *src* property is used in an <img> tag. You can use absolute or relative positioning for this.

An example of the complete <link> tag for the stylesheet you have defined for the sample site is:

```
<link rel="stylesheet" type="text/css"
href="Include/styles.css" />
```

The <link> tag is most often placed between the <head> tags for a page. You can define styles inside the <body> tag, but this is not a recommended practice.

ACTIVITY 4.4 – CREATING AN EXTERNAL STYLE SHEET

For this activity, you will cut and paste the styles that you have defined for your site into an external style sheet. You should replace the entire <style> block within your page with a <link> tag to the new style sheet you have created. You should make sure to place your external style sheet in an **Include** folder within your main project folder. The file extension for the external CSS file should be .css. You can test the results in a Web browser to be sure you have done this correctly.

CHAPTER SUMMARY

In this chapter, you learned how to define style sets in CSS for tags, classes, and IDs. You learned when each of these should be invoked and how to reuse each. The standard format of CSS style commands was covered and practiced, and you should now be able to read and understand CSS code, as well as use the properties covered in this chapter. If you have followed along with the sample layout code, your page content should be as follows (prior to creation of the external style sheet):

```
<!DOCTYPE html>
<html>
    <head>
        <title>Zippy Beans Coffee Co.</title>
        <style type="text/css">
            body {
                margin-left: 0px;
                margin-right: 0px;
                margin-top: 0px;
                margin-bottom: 0px;
                height: 100%;
                width: 100%;
                background-color: #E0FFD1;
                background-attachment: fixed;
                background-repeat: no-repeat;
                background-image: linear-↵
gradient(left top, #4BE60E 2%, #E0FFD1 65%);
                background-image: -o-linear-↵
gradient(left top, #4BE60E 2%, #E0FFD1 65%);
                background-image: -moz-linear- ↵
gradient(left top, #4BE60E 2%, #E0FFD1 65%);
                background-image: -webkit- ↵
linear-gradient(left top, #4BE60E 2%, #E0FFD1 65%);
                background-image: -ms-linear-↵
```

```
gradient(left top, #4BE60E 2%, #E0FFD1 65%);
                        background-image: -webkit-⏎
gradient(

                                linear,
                                left top,
                                right bottom,
                                color-stop(0.02, #4BE60E),
                                color-stop(0.65, #E0FFD1)
                        );
                        font-family: arial, helvetica, ⏎
sans-serif;
                        font-size: 12pt;
                }


                .grad {
                        background-image: linear- ⏎
gradient(left top, #4BE60E 2%, #E0FFD1 65%);
                        background-image: -o-linear- ⏎
gradient(left top, #4BE60E 2%, #E0FFD1 65%);
                        background-image: -moz-linear- ⏎
gradient(left top, #4BE60E 2%, #E0FFD1 65%);
                        background-image: -webkit- ⏎
linear-gradient(left top, #4BE60E 2%, #E0FFD1 65%);
                        background-image: -ms-linear- ⏎
gradient(left top, #4BE60E 2%, #E0FFD1 65%);
                        background-image: -webkit- ⏎
gradient(

                                linear,
                                left top,
                                right bottom,
                                color-stop(0.02, #4BE60E),
                                color-stop(0.65, #E0FFD1)
                        );

                }
```

```
#banner {
        position: fixed;
        top: 0px;
        left: 0px;
        z-index: 30;
        width: 100%;
        height: 130px;
        padding-left: 200px;
        padding-top: 10px;
        padding-right: 10px;
        background-image:url('./Media/ ↵
banner.png');
        background-repeat:no-repeat;
        background-position: top;
        background-size: 100% 130px;
        color: #fff;
        font-family: 'Bauhaus 93';
        font-size: 36pt;
        text-shadow: 2pt 2pt 4pt #020;
}
#logo {
        position: fixed;
        top: 0px;
        left: 0px;
        z-index: 40;
        height: 175px;
        width: 175px;
        margin-left: 20px;
        text-align: center;
}
#logo_img {
        height: 150px;
        width: 150px;
}
```

```css
#logo_img:hover {
        height: 175px;
        width: 175px;
}
#menu {
        position: fixed;
        top: 80px;
        left: 220px;
        z-index: 20;
        width: 780px;
        height: 30px;
        padding-top: 50px;
        padding-left: 8px;
        padding-bottom: -4px;
        background-color: #3c3;
        color: #efe;
        border-bottom-left-radius: 16px;
        border-bottom-right-radius: 16px;
        box-shadow: 2px 2px 6px 0px #030;
        -webkit-box-shadow: 2px 2px  ↵
6px   0px #030;
        text-align: left;
        font-size: 10pt;
}
#cup {
        position: fixed;
        top: 160px;
        left: 0px;
        z-index: 10;
}
#cup_img {
        width: 220px;
        height: 306px;
}
```

```
#content {
        position: absolute;
        top: 140px;
        left: 200px;
        width: 800px;
        background-color: #fff;
        padding-left: 20px;
        padding-right: 20px;
        padding-top: 35px;
        padding-bottom: 20px;
        color: #010;
        background-color: #fff;
        border-radius: 16px;
        text-shadow: 1px 1px 2px ↵
rgba(0,10,0,0.2);;
        }
#bottom {
        position: fixed;
        bottom: 0px;
        left: 0px;
        z-index: 30;
        width: 100%;
        height: 80px;
        padding-left: 10px;
        padding-right: 10px;
        padding-top: 30px;
        background-image:url('./Media/ ↵
footer.png');
        background-repeat:no-repeat;
        background-size: 100% 80px;
        background-position: bottom;
        color: #fff;
        }
    </style>
```

```
    </head>
    <body class="grad">
        <div id="banner" name="banner">Banner</div>
        <div id="logo" name="logo"><img id=" ↵
logo_img" alt="Zippy Beans Logo" src="Media/logo.
png" /></div>
        <div id="menu" name="menu">Menu</div>
        <div id="cup" name="cup"><img id="cup_img" ↵
alt="Zippy Beans Cup" src="Media/cup.png" /></div>
        <div id="content" name="content">Content ↵
</div>
        <div id="bottom" name="bottom">Bottom</div>
    </body>
</html>
```

Figure 4.1 shows a comparison of the initial visual prototype with the implemented results in Mozilla Firefox using this code.

▲ *FIGURE 4.1* Comparison of Initial Visual Prototype (top) and Implemented Results (bottom)

You should take this time to create the external style sheet for your projects so you have an easy place to refine elements as you complete your front-end site design in the next chapter. That chapter will focus on additional HTML elements to include in your page, content planning, and site finalization. The rest of the book (Chapters 6 through 8) focuses on implementing dynamic content and handling user actions on the site.

CHAPTER KNOWLEDGE CHECK

1 Which of the following CSS properties does not affect element positioning?

- ○ **A.** position
- ○ **B.** top
- ○ **C.** left
- ○ **D.** layer
- ○ **E.** None of the above

2 Which of the following is an incorrect label for a style set in CSS?

- ○ **A.** #img { ... }
- ○ **B.** .img { ... }
- ○ **C.** img { ... }
- ○ **D.** img { ... }

3 Which of the following values are not accepted by the *position* property?

- ○ **A.** absolute
- ○ **B.** relative
- ○ **C.** inline
- ○ **D.** static
- ○ **E.** None of the above

4 The greater the difference in *z-index* values, the greater the visual depth of the layers will become.

- ○ **A.** True
- ○ **B.** False

5

The following are accepted values for *height* for an element except:

○ **A.** 100%

○ **B.** 10px

○ **C.** 10em

○ **D.** 1%

○ **E.** None of the above

6

The _____ defines the distance between an element and its nearest allowed neighbor.

○ **A.** spacing

○ **B.** padding

○ **C.** margin

○ **D.** buffer

7

The property *background*_____ defines how the background tiles within the boundaries of an element.

○ **A.** width

○ **B.** attachment

○ **C.** repeat

○ **D.** image

○ **E.** All of the above

○ **F.** None of the above

8

The style command nearest to the HTML tag takes precedence for display.

○ **A.** True

○ **B.** False

9

Which of the following properties governs the application of italic text?

○ **A.** font-size

○ **B.** font-weight

○ **C.** text-style

○ **D.** text-decoration

10 Which of the following is an incorrect color declaration in CSS?

○ **A.** #fef
○ **B.** #ddffee
○ **C.** rgb(1,1,10)
○ **D.** rgba(10,10,10,0.5)
○ **E.** All of the above
○ **F.** None of the above

CHAPTER PROJECTS

Project 1: Personal Web Site

For your project in this chapter, you should construct the external style sheet for your site to adjust the initial HTML so it is displayed according to your visual prototype. While you have only one page now, it will be imperative to have an external style sheet before the next chapter, so you can adjust global settings and styles quickly and have them apply to all pages. Make sure to save and test your work in a Web browser.

Project 2: Resort Web Site

For your project in this chapter, you should construct the external style sheet for your site to adjust the initial HTML so it is displayed according to your visual prototype. While you have only one page now, it will be imperative to have an external style sheet before the next chapter, so you can adjust global settings and styles quickly and have them apply to all pages. Make sure to save and test your work in a Web browser.

CHAPTER EXERCISES

1. Give an example of when you would use a style set on a tag name, a class to be invoked, and a single ID within a document. Explain the reason for this choice in each circumstance.

2. How would you represent the color *#0f0* in two-character hexadecimal format, RGB format, and RGBA format? Explain your answer.

3. What is the maximum number of style commands (or style sets) that can affect the following tag (assuming no external style sheet):

```
<div id="mydiv" name="mydiv" style="font-weight:
bold;">
```
Explain your answer.

4. Create a style set for a bold, 10pt, sans-serif font with a text shadow that will apply to every <div> tag in a page. Explain your answer.

5. Create a style set for white text over a background mixing pure green with pure blue; define it to apply as a class.

6. Describe two reasons that comments are needed in CSS. Give an example of both uses.

7. If a single tag has an external style sheet, a <style> tag within the page, a style set defined for its ID, a class, and a style attribute, which of these would take precedence if the same style property were defined multiple times? Explain your answer.

8. Explain why it may be useful to define a style set for a tag ID and still invoke a class for that tag.

9. Create a class for headers in a page using at least six style attributes. Describe how the contents of the tag will appear in the page when the class is called.

10. The use of the style attribute in HTML elements should be limited to absolute necessity. Explain why using this attribute undercuts some of the power and usefulness of CSS. Justify your position.

CHAPTER REVIEW QUESTIONS

1. Explain briefly why it is important to separate the display of elements within a page from the structure of elements within a page. Justify your answer.

2. Briefly explain the benefits of inheritance in style sheets. How does this save effort and centralize style commands? Justify your answer.

3. Explain why it is important for older browsers to "fail gracefully" and ignore a style command that they do not recognize. What would be the consequences if the browser did not have this behavior? Justify your answer.

4. Explain the purpose of altering a style set on a hyperlink when a user hovers the mouse over it. What benefit does this provide the user?

5. Explain the benefits of using an external style sheet for a site. Are there any negative consequences to using this type of CSS? Justify your answer.

6. Explain the purpose of an anchor point in element display. Why are the corners good candidates for anchor points? What factors affect the choice of a corner for an anchor point?

7. Which aspect of CSS is more important to the presentation of content on a Web site, positioning or display? Explain your position.

8. Why are borders a better troubleshooting tool for CSS than setting a background color? Explain your answer.

9. Briefly explain the purpose of listing multiple fonts in a *font-family* value. What is the drawback of not defining multiple fonts in this list? Justify your position.

10. Briefly define the concept of an elastic measurement in CSS. What are three of the possible applications of this type of measurement unit?

HTML5

This chapter ends the design phase of the site and moves into content creation and establishing functionality. As part of this chapter, you will establish a firm site map so you can plan the navigation correctly. You will also incorporate hyperlinks for creating a fully connected and functional site. This chapter also includes an expansion of the HTML tag usage you have already learned to facilitate content creation and presentation on the individual site pages using HTML version 5 (or HTML5). Once you have completed this chapter, you should be able to:

- Create a site map for a project and establish consistent branding of pages

- Add hyperlinks and image hotspots to establish page connectivity

- Add content to a page, including line breaks, tables, and forms

- Add multimedia elements to your site, including video, audio, and plug-in content

5.1 BRANDING A SITE

One of the most important things on a Web site is consistency of elements across all of the pages of the site. Maintaining this consistency helps to establish the professionalism and credibility of your site. This is an essential element of presentation on any site, and it is one of the reasons the careful creation of a visual prototype is such a worthwhile exercise. Establishing consistent navigation and making sure you have working links is necessary for any site. Users are driven away from any site with even a single broken link; this will destroy any credibility on the site regardless of how much effort was put into the display or the content.

5.1.1 Planning for Content

The next exercise that you need to complete as you move forward in the visual presentation of the site is establishing the pages of content you will have. This will allow you to construct a consistent navigation strategy for your site so users can find content easily when they go from page to page within the site. It is important to make sure the content of a single page is all very closely related. Any content that extends below the bottom of the screen (requiring the user to scroll) should be structured so that the important information is listed at the top and users are required to scroll down only if they are interested in the content that is lower on the current page. You also want to make sure that your Web pages are clearly identified and that the text linking to the Web page is closely associated with the link text for clarity.

For this text, you will establish a consistent navigation strategy for your pages in the project. In more advanced sites, you can dynamically generate the navigation text and even make it context sensitive. Doing this generally requires either JavaScript or a back-end server-side language like PHP or PERL.

5.1.2 Creating a Site Map

When planning content, you should establish a clear site map for the project. This should detail the title of the page, the name of the file for the page, and the pages to which it is connected. You should establish each page based on the content it will include (based on the content that is essential to present) and group together similar pages that will be linked to it. The homepage (which should be the *index.html* file) should have a substantial enough number of links in the navigation to reach all of the pages in the site through some path of links. You should also strive to minimize the number of clicks to reach a destination.

It is a careful balancing act to determine how large to make your navigation system to minimize the number of clicks needed to reach a destination. A navigation panel that is too large can be overwhelming to a user, but taking too many clicks to reach a page will deter users as well. There is no precise solution for any of this, but context-sensitive menus and expanding menus are options to reduce the number of clicks and still preserve a small navigation area on the page. These are more advanced topics than introductory HTML and support-ing languages. Courses or books on human-computer interface will help in this regard.

You can use PowerPoint to create a site map, just as you did to cre-ate your initial visual prototype. The rectangle shapes and the lines you used then are good for constructing a map of content pages for the site. You should start with the homepage (*index.html*) and expand the content links from that. You can see an example of a site map in Figure 5.1.

For the sample project, you will construct four pages, including the homepage. The homepage will include the content about the company. The additional pages will include a contact page, a menu of bever-ages and/or food, and a page with directions and hours. For most sites, the navigation system would be much more extensive than this and

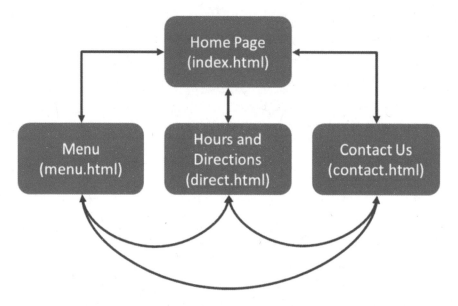

▲ **FIGURE 5.1** Site Map for the Sample Project

would have different levels. The sample projects for this text while you are getting started all have simple navigation with a small number of pages.

ACTIVITY 5.1 – CREATING A SITE MAP

For this activity, you will plan one additional page for the sample project and construct a site map that includes all of the sample pages and the new content page you have planned. You can use PowerPoint to construct this page, but you should be sure to include the name of the file as well as the title of the page.

5.1.3 Hyperlinks

One of the most essential tools for Web site construction is hyperlinks. A hyperlink in terms of Web pages is a connection between resources, commonly used to link one page to another or to link sections within a page. The tags for this are the anchor tags, <a> and </a>. There are two uses for a hyperlink: to link to a resource outside the page (external referencing) and to provide a connection to a bookmark within the same page (ID referencing). The *href* (or *hyper-reference*) attribute is used for both. Like the *src* attribute in <img> tags, *href* can use both relative and absolute addressing. Any text between the <a> and </a> tags will be activated as the link, which activates the connection to the reference when clicked. An example of this is:

```
<a href="contact.html">Contact Us!</a>
```

Clicking the text "Contact Us!" using the mouse will take the user to the contact page.

To use the *href* attribute for a link within the page, the target section must be tagged with its ID. Any tag (such as <div>) with an *id* attribute in it can be targeted using the <a> tag. For the reference to be activated, the tag with the *id* attribute must be below the content visible in the browser window. In the *href* attribute, you can simply precede the value of the ID you want to reference with a # symbol. An example of this is:

```
<a href="#myid">Bookmark</a>
...
<img id="myid" ... />
```

You can also use a combination of external referencing and ID referencing by adding a link to the page followed by a hash symbol and the ID you wish to reference.

5.1.4 Image Links/Hotspots

In addition to text, you can also wrap an image tag in anchor tags to allow the image to act as a link. An example of this is:

```
<a href="index.html"><img src="Media/logo.png"
alt="Zippy Beans"></a>
```

This will cause the entire image to act as a link. Combining this with the previous description of the anchor tags, the hyperlink navigation code for the sample project should be:

```
<body>
```

```
        ...
        <div id="logo" name="logo"><a href=" ↵
index.html"><img id="logo_img" alt="Zippy Beans ↵
Logo" src="Media/logo.png" /></a> </div>
        <div id="menu" name="menu"><a href="menu. ↵
html">Menu</a> | <a href="direct.html">Hours and ↵
Directions</a> | <a href="contact.html">Contact ↵
Us!</a></div>
        ...
    </body>
```

When you view this in a browser, you will see that by default the display of any hyperlinked text is to display as blue with an underline. Visited links by default display as underlined purple text. You can change this appearance by creating a CSS command set for the anchor tag that sets the *color* and *text-decoration* values.

You can also use *hotspots* to link pieces of an image. Hotspots are clickable sections of an image defined through an image map; most Web authoring tools have the ability to create these easily. This is useful for large images that you want to map to multiple locations. The most common types of hotspots are rectangles and circles, but it is also possible to define your own custom hotspots point by point.

In some browsers, wrapping an image tag with anchor tags will cause the image to have a border displayed around it. To eliminate this, you can add the CSS command **border: 0;** to the style definition for the <img> tag.

The easiest way to establish hotspots in a page is to use a Web design tool like Adobe Dreamweaver or Microsoft Expression Web. In Dreamweaver, the Hotspot tool is located in the Insert panel at the upper right corner of the interface; from here, you can select a rectangular, oval, or polygon hotspot (where you define your own point set to create an enclosed polygon). In Expression Web, the Pictures toolbar must be activated to access the tools for creating hotspots. To activate the toolbar, select View, Toolbars, and then Pictures. With the Pictures toolbar active, select an image to activate the options and then choose the Rectangular Hotspot, the Circular Hotspot, or the Polygonal Hotspot tool.

The common expectation in modern Web sites is to click the logo of the page to return to the homepage of the site. You should make sure to provide this functionality either by linking your entire logo image to the homepage or by creating a hotspot within your banner to allow a user to go back to the start of the site.

With the Pictures tool active, you can simply draw the shape on the image to create the hotspot. A series of prompts will appear, asking you to provide the link and alternative text information for each hotspot you create. The code generated by this will look as follows:

```
<map name="Map" id="Map">
<area shape="circle" coords="56,48,36" href="index.↵
html" alt="Home Page" />
</map>
```

You can create this code manually, but it requires knowing exactly where you want the shape placed and the pixel coordinates of its vertices and/or radius distance.

ACTIVITY 5.2 – CONSTRUCTING NAVIGATION ELEMENTS

For this activity, you will alter the index.html page for your project to add hyperlinked navigation elements for each of the included pages. You should add an image link around the logo to link to index.html. You should also add links to the <div> tag for navigation to each of the pages in your site individually. Be sure to define a CSS style set for the anchor tag, so the hyperlink text will be displayed correctly on your page. You can also adjust the width of the menu element to account for the size of the navigation system.

5.1.5 Meta Tags

Another support tag that you should consider for your site is the <meta> tag, which is used to provide information about the site. (*meta information is information about information.*) These tags appear inside the page header (between the <head> and </head> tags). The common attributes used in a <meta> tag are *name* and *content*. The *name* attribute specifies the type of <meta> tag, and the *content* attribute specifies the value associated with the *name* attribute. An example of this is:

```
<meta name="author" content="Dr. Theodor ↵
Richardson">
```

There are a number of common <meta> tags that can be used to provide site information. Some of the common <meta> tag names are:

- *description:* The content item for this is a text description of the page and its contents.

- *author:* The content item for this is the name of the page author.

- *keywords:* The content item for this is a comma-separated list of key terms by which the page should be identified by search engines.

- *robots:* This is a *de facto* standard for whether pages will be indexed by a search bot (like those used by Google) or whether the links in the page will be followed for further site exploration. The default value for this is "index, follow," allowing search bots to index the page and follow the links in it. To disallow one or the other, just add *no* in front of the term. A full exclusion would be "noindex, nofollow," but you can also specify these values independently (such as "index, nofollow").

Meta information is helpful for search engine optimization, allowing your site to be visited by search engine bots (called spiders) and catalogued according to the meta information you provide. Without this meta information, the initial text content of the page will be displayed in the search results for most search engines that find your page.

5.1.6 Cloning Pages

At this point, you should finalize your content for the *index.html* page, including any content that will be common to all pages. For instance, in the sample case project page, you still need to add the banner text and the disclaimer text. With the subheading of the banner text (shown in the visual prototype for the case project) and the disclaimer placement, you need to add two new <div> elements to accomplish this.

Remember that new tags should be introduced only for structural elements. Since the subheading has to be formatted differently from the banner text and the disclaimer has to be positioned within the footer, both of these additions fall into this category.

With the added <div> tags, CSS definitions, and content for these common elements, the code for your *index.html* page should be:

```
<head>
        <title>Zippy Beans Coffee Co.</title>
        <style type="text/css">
            ...
            a {
                    color: #fff;
                    text-decoration: none;
            }
            #menu a {
                    background-color: #3c3;
                    border-radius: 4px;
            }
            #disclaimer {
                    margin-top: 40px;
                    font-size: 8pt;
            }
```

```
                    #subhead {
                         font-size: 22pt;

                    }
          </style>
     </head>
     <body class="grad">
          <div id="banner" name="banner">Zippy Beans ⏎
Coffee Co.<div id="subhead">Totally Organic, Man!</
div></div>
          ...
          <div id="bottom" name="bottom"><div id= ⏎
"disclaimer">This is a fictional company. No coffee ⏎
beans were harmed in the making of this site.<div> ⏎
</div>
     </body>
```

Figure 5.2 shows the result of adding these new <div> elements. This should be your final *index.html* if you have followed along with the examples so far.

▲ **FIGURE 5.2** Completed *index.html* File

An important part of branding your site is creating pages that have elements in exactly the same place from page to page. Fortunately, this also saves you work. You can use your *index.html* page as a template for the rest of your site. To do this, simply use the Save As functionality in whatever software program you are using to write your HTML, and name the file with the filename of one of the other pages in the site from your site map. This is known as cloning the page. Repeat this process for every page you wish to create. When you are finished, you should have every page listed in your site map as an identical file within your project folder. For the example, this would mean cloning *index.html* into *menu.html*, *contact.html*, and *direct.html*. To finish each page, all you need to do is add content specific to each of the pages individually.

You may notice the style entry for **#menu** a in the sample code in this section. This is an example of a complex class that applies only to <a> tags within the <div> tag with the ID value **menu**. This can be a powerful way to format elements within other elements without calling each of them by name or invoking classes in every tag.

5.1.7 Adding a Site Icon

You may notice when browsing different Web sites that professional sites have an icon to the left of the site name. This is created by a file called *favicon.ico* in the root directory of the site. (This is default behavior, with more complex alternatives available.) This adds a great finishing touch to a site, even if it is a personal site. The quickest way to create one of these icons for your site is to use a Web application at *http://www.favicon.cc* called *favicon.ico Generator*. This application allows you to create a favicon pixel by pixel or to import an image. You can see an example of the imported logo for the case project in the pixel grid on Figure 5.3.

▲ **FIGURE 5.3** Sample favicon.ico for the Case Project

When you have finished your icon, make sure to save it as *favi-con.ico* in the root folder (your project folder) for your site. You can do this by selecting the *Download Favicon* link at the bottom of the icon display. These icons may not be displayed when you are viewing your local copy, but they should be displayed once your site is hosted on a Web server.

ACTIVITY 5.3 – FINAL SITE BRANDING

For this activity, you will finalize the index.html page for your project (with any remaining common elements needed) and clone it into the rest of the pages established in your site map. At this point, you should make use of an external style sheet if you have not already done this. **Remember to update the image links in the style commands if you change the folder in which your styles are kept.** This centralizes your style commands so they can all be changed in one place when you have multiple pages using the same style set. You should also create a **favicon.ico** file for your site. This will prepare you to complete the content pages as the final activity of this chapter. Be sure to include the additional content page you created for the site map exercise.

5.2 ADDING CONTENT

Now that your site is branded and you have all of your pages linked via your navigation system, it is time to add content to your site. If you have followed the steps of planning so far, this should be one of the easiest steps in the process. For each page you created, you should add the content that is necessary and relevant for that page. If a user must scroll to view it all, it should be a continuation of what is presented in the initial window rather than a new topic that must be found. This process will begin with adding content to the *index.html* page, which will be a company description. If you have a photo to advertise the business (such as a storefront) this page would be a good place to add that as well.

5.2.1 Using Paragraphs and Line Breaks

For the main page in the sample site, the only content needed is text describing the business and its philosophy and history. The way to separate text into paragraphs is to wrap each paragraph in <p> and </p> tags. This will automatically add space before and after the text and end the last line at the closing </p> tag. You can see an example of this here:

```
<div id="content" name="content"><p>Welcome to ↵
Zippy Beans! Our company is committed to the ↵
greenest technologies available to deliver you the ↵
finest, freshest cup of coffee you have ever had!</p>
<p>Our factory has one of the highest smog outputs ↵
of any organization in the world, and we are proud ↵
to say that we plant trees to make up for every ↵
single carbon emission. By 2014, we will have to ↵
plant trees within trees to make up for this ↵
deficit, and that will be exciting to see!</p>
<p>Join us in Times Square for a fresh, fast, ↵
overpriced cup of our delicious, eco-friendly, ↵
totally organic, highly caffeinated coffee! We ↵
hope you have a zippy day!</p></div>
```

Remember that you can control the behavior of the <p> tag with CSS commands. This includes setting indents and margins for the text within the paragraph tag wrapper.

If you need to manually insert a line break, you can do so with a <br /> tag. (
 is also commonly acceptable but is considered improper form for the stricter document type XHTML.) Like the <img> tag, this tag has no closing, so the closing mark is included before the end of the tag itself to signify that it has no partner tag. You should use the <br /> tag only to end lines as needed rather than to create individual paragraphs. For that, you should use the <p> and </p> tags. You can see an example of this for creating a signature line in the *index.html* page of the sample project:

```
<div id="content" name="content"><p>Welcome to ↵
  Zippy Beans! … We hope you have a zippy day! ↵
</p>Sincerely,<br />The Zippy Team</div>
```

5.2.2 Ampersand Commands

One of the issues with using HTML is white space. Any consecutive white space is treated as a single blank character space. This means you can add blank lines, spaces, and tabs in your source document and the only display effect will be a single blank letter space. To add specific spacing, you can use a tool called an *ampersand command* (also called a *character entity* in HTML). These commands begin with the ampersand (&) character and end with a semicolon (;). For a non-breaking space, the ampersand command is * * to display a single blank space. You can add multiple ampersand commands to force spacing. Adding *   * to your document will add five consecutive white spaces to the text.

There are other useful ampersand commands. For instance, any less than (<) or greater than (>) characters in HTML will be parsed as tags, so if you want these characters to be displayed in your content, you can use the ampersand commands *<* and *>*, respectively, to display them. Other unique characters, like the copyright symbol, can be created using ampersand commands (in this case, ©). These can also be used to create foreign language characters and currency notations in text display. A complete reference for ampersand commands is provided at the Webmonkey Web site: *http://www.webmonkey.com/2010/02/special_characters.*

Unlike the case with HTML tags, capitalization does matter in ampersand commands just as it does in simple text. There are diacritics marks which can apply to either the lowercase or uppercase character and will need to be capitalized correctly to display the correct variant.

5.2.3 Adding Tables

Tables in HTML are added with the <table> and </table> tags. Tables are divided into rows (which use the <tr> and </tr> tags) and then into cells (which use the <td> and </td> tags). To create a table with two rows and three columns, the code is:

```
<table>
    <tr>
        <td>1</td>
<td>2</td>
<td>3</td>
    </tr>
    <tr>
        <td>4</td>
<td>5</td>
<td>6</td>
    </tr>
</table>
```

Just like <div> tags, <table> tags can be nested inside each other. To do this, you just need to start and end the table inside a single table data cell of the original table.

The easiest way to insert a table into an HTML document is using a visual editor like Adobe Dreamweaver or Microsoft Expression Web. To do this, select the Insert menu and choose Table in Adobe Dreamweaver; for Expression Web, select the Table menu and choose Insert Table. From here you can add a table based on the number of rows and columns you wish it to have. You can see an example of this in Figure 5.4.

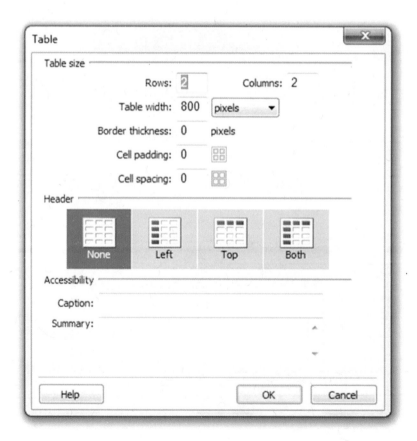

▲ **FIGURE 5.4** Sample Dialog for Table Creation

You can merge cells within a table using the *rowspan* and *colspan* attributes. The *rowspan* attribute merges the specified number of cells across a row. The *colspan* attribute merges the specified number of cells down a column. Table cells are ordered left to right in the specified table row. You can omit the <td> tags for cells that have been incorporated into a merge. You can see an example of cell merging in a table here:

```
<table>
    <tr>
        <td colspan="2">1 and 2</td>
        <!-- This table cell is combined into cell⏎
  1 and 2 -->
        <td rowspan="2">3 and 6</td>
    </tr>
    <tr>
        <td>4</td>
        <td>5</td>
        <!-- This table cell is combined into ⏎
  cell 3 and 6 -->
    </tr>
</table>
```

A comment in HTML begins with <!-- and ends with -->. Anything between these will be ignored by the browser but can still be seen by a user viewing the source code for the page.

You can control table display with CSS commands, just as you can control the display of other elements. The CSS commands *text-align* and *vertical-align* control the horizontal and vertical placement of content within <td> tags. Inside the <table> tag, you can place attributes for *cellpadding* (the distance between cell walls and content) and *cell-*

spacing (the distance between cells). You can see these together in the content for the *menu.html* page for the sample case project:

```
<div id="content" name="content">
  <table cellspacing="0" cellpadding="4">
        <tr>
              <td></td>
              <td>Mini-Large</td>
              <td>Large</td>
              <td>Gallons</td>
        </tr>
        <tr>
              <td>Zippy Coffee</td>
              <td>$3.50</td>
              <td>$3.75</td>
              <td>$15.50</td>
        </tr>
        <tr>
              <td>Zippyccino</td>
              <td>$4.50</td>
              <td>$5.50</td>
              <td>$27.50</td>
        </tr>
        <tr>
              <td>Zippy Mochaccino</td>
              <td>$5.50</td>
              <td>$6.50</td>
              <td>$29.50</td>
        </tr>
        <tr>
              <td>Double Zippyspresso</td>
              <td>$3.50</td>
              <td>$4.50</td>
              <td>$25.50</td>
```

```
            </tr>
            <tr>
                    <td>Zippy Macchiatoccino</td>
                    <td>$7.50</td>
                    <td>$8.50</td>
                    <td>$45.50</td>
            </tr>
        </table>
    </div>
```

You can use CSS commands to control the **cellpadding** and **cellspacing** in a <table> tag, but this is one instance in which it is recommended that you use the HTML attributes for formatting. The CSS alternative for **cellspacing** (the **border-collapse** command) is not well supported across browsers, and it will be overridden by the value of the HTML attribute anyway. The padding CSS command can be used in place of **cellpadding** tag attribute if you are defining table styles already, but the **padding** style command should be applied to the <tr> and <td> tags.

5.2.4 Adding Forms

Forms are one of the most efficient and effective ways to gather user feedback and provide interactivity on a Web site. Forms have a variety of inputs that can be incorporated, but to function correctly and submit their values when the form is submitted, they all must be wrapped within the same <form> and </form> tags. The <form> tag has a number of attributes that determine how the form behaves when a user submits it:

- *name:* This is the name of the form. It is important to add this attribute so the form can be referenced by JavaScript and back-end languages like PHP.

- *action:* This defines the location to which the form data should be sent when the form is submitted. This is typically a back-end server language page or a servlet.

- *method:* This attribute has two common values, POST and GET. POST submits the form data to the action destination as a packet. GET places the information in the query string after the action address in a URL; this is the less secure and less common way to process forms.

You can see an example of the form wrapper here:

```
<form name="contact" action="contact.php"
method="POST">

    ...

</form>
```

There are a number of different types of input that can be added to a form. Most of these use the <input> tag. The common attributes for the <input> tag are *name*, *type*, and *value*. The *name* attribute uniquely identifies the input within the form. The *value* attribute is used to provide an initial value for the form or the selection value for checkboxes and radio buttons. The common values for the *type* attribute are as follows:

- *text:* This is a standard text box for data entry.

- *password:* This is the same as a text entry, but it hides the user input from view for entries such as a password that have to be kept secret.

- *radio:* This type codes for a radio button, a selection method that allows the user to choose only one item from a list. The *name* attribute should be the same for every entry in the same radio button group. A *value* attribute must be used for each radio button.

- *checkbox:* A checkbox is similar to a radio button, but it allows users to select multiple items within a list. Checkbox items can be individually named, or they can be named as a group.

- *hidden:* The hidden input type is a way to retain a value within a form without displaying it as part of the page content. The *name* and *value* attributes are what make this input type useful, since a user cannot directly modify the contents of this field. Remember that the user can see the contents of this field when viewing the source code for the page.

- *submit:* The submit type creates a "Submit" button for the form, which sends the form input to the destination identified by the form's *action* attribute. The value attribute for a *submit* input type will be the text displayed on the button.

You can see an example of these in the following code:

```
<form name="contact" action="contact.php" ⏎
method="POST">
Name: <input type="text" name="myname"><br />
  Email: <input type="text" name="email"><br />
  Preferred Method of Contact: <br />
  <input type="radio" name="preference" ⏎
value="Email">Email<br />
  <input type="radio" name="preference" ⏎
value="Phone">Phone<br />
  <input type="checkbox" name="subscribe" ⏎
value="Yes">Subscribe to the Zippy Beans ⏎
newsletter!<br />
  <input type="submit" value="Submit!">
</form>
```

There are two additional form input types that can be added. These are the text area and the selection box. A text area is similar to a text input, but it allows multiple rows of text in a single entry. This is good for user input that is longer, such as the content of a contact form. The tags for a text area are <textarea> and </textarea>. The attributes for a text area are *name*, *cols*, and *rows*. The *cols* attribute defines how many character widths across the text area box will be, and *rows* defines how many rows of input will be shown at one time. The text can overflow beyond the *rows* and *cols* attribute parameters. Any text that appears between the opening and closing tags for the text area will be displayed as a value for the field. An example of the code for the text area is:

```
Message:<br />
<textarea name="message" rows="4" cols="50"></.
textarea><br />
```

The selection type for form input works differently from other form input types. The listed items each have their own tag within a wrapper of <select> and </select>. The <select> tag just requires a *name* attribute. Each possible value is wrapped in <option> and </option> tags. The <option> tag has to have a *value* attribute which defines the value of the selection when that option is chosen. You can add the standalone attribute (one with no value pairing) *selected* to one of the <option> tags to give it a default value. You can see an example of a selection tag for salutations here:

```
<select name="salutation">
    <option value="Miss">Miss</option>
    <option value="Mrs">Mrs.</option>
    <option value="Ms">Ms.</option>
    <option value="Mr">Mr.</option>
    <option value="Dr" selected>Dr.</option>
    <option value="Sir">Sir</option>
    <option value="Madam">Madam</option>
</select>
```

To put all of this together, the code for the contact form (on the *contact.html* page) for the sample case project should be:

```
<div id="content" name="content">
    <form name="contact" action="contact.php" ↵
method="POST">
        Name:
        <select name="salutation">
            <option value="Miss">Miss</option>
            <option value="Mrs">Mrs.</option>
            <option value="Ms">Ms.</option>
            <option value="Mr">Mr.</option>
            <option value="Dr" selected>Dr.↵
</option>
            <option value="Sir">Sir</option>
            <option value="Madam">Madam</option>
```

```
            </select>
            <input type="text" name="myname"><br />
            Email: <input type="text" name="email">↵
<br />
            Preferred Method of Contact: <br />
            <input type="radio" name="preference" ↵
value="Email"> Email<br />
            <input type="radio" name="preference" ↵
value="Phone"> Phone<br />
            <input type="checkbox" name="subscribe" ↵
value="Yes"> Subscribe to the Zippy Beans ↵
newsletter!<br />
            Message:<br />
            <textarea name="message" rows="4" ↵
cols="50"></textarea><br />
            <input type="submit" value="Submit!">
        </form>
    </div>
```

If you preview the form with this code, everything will be displayed correctly, but it will not be formatted nicely. In order to control the display of your form elements, you should consider placing them in a table. This will allow for consistent spacing and alignment of the form entries and the descriptive text. It is a worthwhile practice exercise to convert the form for the sample project to a table layout.

5.2.5 Audio and Video

In HTML5, the incorporation of audio and video into your Web pages has become very easy. This used to require the support of complex code or external plug-ins which have limited support and require user installation. Now you can simply use the <audio> and <video> tags to add this content. The preferred format for audio is *MP3,* and the preferred format for video is *MP4*. Most audio and video construction software packages support these formats. The source file for either an audio or video element should be referenced for this tag using a single <source> tag. You can see an example of these tags here:

```
<audio controls="controls">
<source src="example.mp3" type="audio/mp3" />
</audio>


<video width="320" height="240" controls="controls">
<source src="example.mp4" type="video/mp4" />
</video>
```

There are a variety of options available, such as playback controls and features you can add for the audio and video content. You can also set the content to play automatically (*autoplay*) or loop. You can set the height and width for the display of the video as well. You should allow your users to have as much control as possible over the content, but you should also make it minimally invasive (low emphasis) unless the page is dedicated specifically to that media element. If a browser does not support these tags, whatever content is between the opening and closing tags will be displayed as text content on the page.

NOTE

Unless the site has a specific need for background audio, you should not add this type of sound to your pages. Consider that it will play whenever a user enters the page; it can get obnoxious quickly and will drive users away. With that said, there are sites for which this works, such as band Web sites and sites for movies and games. In general, though, it should be avoided.

5.2.6 Embedded Code

Another case you will likely encounter is the need to embed external content into your pages. Fortunately, most times that this will be necessary, the code will be provided for you. An example of this would be code for adding an Adobe Flash® object (which uses the <object> and <embed> tags) or a video from a site like You-Tube® (*www.youtube.com*). As practice for this, you will use the Google Maps™ application to add a location map to the Hours and Directions page of the case project site. You can start this process at *http://maps.google.com/help/maps/getmaps/*.

You can select any location for the business and find it in Google Maps (*maps.google.com*), then click the icon that looks like a chain to create the link. This will provide you with the ability to customize your map; you can copy the *embed* code provided and paste it into the content of your site (in this case, the *direct.html* page). You should add a one-row, two-column table to the page and place the hours in the left column and the embedded map in the right one.

Using embed codes is common for external content, custom objects, and widgets. Most plug-ins will generate specific HTML code for using them in your page. One thing you should remember is to test the code in multiple browsers to be sure it is displayed correctly.

ACTIVITY 5.4 - CREATING CONTENT

For this activity, you will construct the content for the pages of the case project. This should include all of the pages from the sample site map, as well as the page you created to add to the project information. You can change any of the information given for these pages, but you should be sure to practice using the tags to create the specified content. Be sure to consider the display of your content as well and add CSS style sets as needed to format your display. Be sure to test your pages in multiple browsers.

CHAPTER SUMMARY

This chapter concluded the creation of the static content for your site. This represents the initial functional prototype for the site. The next step is to implement any dynamic content and the processing of the *form* content that you have set up in this chapter. You may have noticed that the *form* content directs users to a page that has not been created. The next chapter will focus on the JavaScript language and how it can be used to validate input and manipulate display elements. Chapter 7 focuses on form processing and directing content using back-end languages like PHP and PERL. Finally, Chapter 8 covers the integration of MySQL for managing data on a Web site. You should now have the tools to construct almost any page in HTML and format it for display using CSS commands.

CHAPTER KNOWLEDGE CHECK

1 Which of the following is not a valid *type* value for form input?

- ○ **A.** text
- ○ **B.** password
- ○ **C.** radio
- ○ **D.** select
- ○ **E.** None of the above

2 Which of the following attributes of the <table> tag is most difficult to reproduce in CSS?

- ○ **A.** border
- ○ **B.** cellpadding
- ○ **C.** cellspacing
- ○ **D.** colspan
- ○ **E.** None of the above

3 Which of the following attributes is used to merge two adjacent cells in the same line on a table?

○ **A.** rowspan

○ **B.** colspan

○ **C.** merge

○ **D.** mergecells

4 Which of the following is a valid ampersand command?

○ **A.** :

○ **B.**

○ **C.** :nbsp&

○ **D.**

○ **E.** None of the above

5 Which of the following is a valid shape that can be added as an image hotspot?

○ **A.** Rectangle

○ **B.** Oval

○ **C.** Circle

○ **D.** Pentagon

○ **E.** All of the above

○ **F.** None of the above

6 Which of the following tags defines a table cell?

○ **A.** <table>

○ **B.** <td>

○ **C.** <tc>

○ **D.** <th>

○ **E.** All of the above

○ **F.** None of the above

7 Tables can be nested inside of other tables in a page, just as <div> tags can be nested.

○ **A.** True
○ **B.** False

8 Input values outside of a form will not be processed when the form is submitted.

○ **A.** True
○ **B.** False

9 Which of the following tags requires an end tag?

○ **A.** <input>
○ **B.** <img>
○ **C.**
○ **D.** <textarea>
○ **E.** None of the above

10 Which of the following tags are new to HTML5?

○ **A.** <p> and
○ **B.** <audio> and <video>
○ **C.** <img> and <a>
○ **D.** <textarea> and <select>
○ **E.** None of the above

CHAPTER PROJECTS

Project 1: Personal Web Site

For this project, you should create a site map for your personal site. You should plan pages for your site that are relevant and important as individual topics. It is better to have more content on the homepage than to create unnecessary pages. You should choose what to show-case on your site and focus on that. Unnecessary pages will deter an audience, so your site will not promote you as it should. You should focus on the content of this site rather than on its complexity; you will be able to practice complexity with the resort site.

Project 2: Resort Web Site

For this project, you should build out the content for the resort. On this site, you should focus on media (including images and video) and creating engaging content to make the viewer want to travel to the resort. The site branding should be appealing and complex. The branding of this site should be the focus of the project; it is meant to be engaging and enticing to the audience.

CHAPTER EXERCISES

1. Describe two cases in which you would want to use comments in an HTML file. Should these comments ever be allowed to remain in the HTML document even when the site is posted live?

2. Using the Web, research the attributes of the <video> tag. Describe how these could be used to modify how the video content plays. Explain why multiple source files are allowed inside this tag.

3. Using the Web, research the attributes of the <audio> tag. Describe how these could be used to modify how the audio content plays. Explain why multiple source files are allowed inside this tag.

4. Give at least three possible uses for the *hidden* input type in a form. With your examples, consider that a user can view the content of these hidden items when viewing the page's source code.

5. Give three examples of when you would use an ampersand command in an HTML document. Why would the character

not display correctly without the use of this special character format?

6. Use the Web to find at least two <meta> tags that are not mentioned in this chapter. Explain what information they provide about the page and what their purpose is.

7. Radio buttons and selection fields serve a similar purpose in an HTML form. Explain in general terms when you would use one or the other. Justify your position.

8. Table cells can be merged only into rectangular arrangements. Explain the logistics of why this is necessary. What would the consequences be if this could be violated? Describe how the <td> tags would be processed in this case.

9. Explain the benefit of wrapping a form in a table. How does this affect usability as well as display?

10. Use the Web to research the CSS commands to create a first-line indentation for paragraphs. Construct the style set for the <p> tag to enable this functionality.

CHAPTER REVIEW QUESTIONS

1. Why is it a good idea to limit the amount of audio or video used on a page? Are there exceptions to this rule, or is it a constant? Justify your answer.

2. Explain in your own words the benefit of cloning pages for creating all of the initial pages in your site without content. Are there any drawbacks to this technique? Justify your position.

3. What is the purpose of using hyperlinks to reference IDs of tags within the same page? Give at least two examples of when this would be a useful feature on a page. Justify your position.

4. Give an example of when you would need to use the * * ampersand command to explicitly add spaces to a document. Is there any other way this could be accomplished in HTML or CSS?

5. Why is it important to limit the use of plug-in content on a Web page? What risk do you run when adding plug-in content that is not inherently supported by the Web browser itself? Explain your answer.

6. The <th> tag can be used to provide a header row for a table. Use the Web to research this tag and its application. What is the benefit of using this tag? Is this required for formatting a table correctly? Explain your answer.

7. Explain the purpose of a *favicon* in a Web site. Is it important to have one for your own site? Why or why not? Justify your position.

8. Why is it better to format text using paragraph tags rather than simply using line breaks to separate text into sections? Justify your answer.

9. Why is it important to adhere to a site map once it has been established? What steps would have to be taken to add a new page of content later?

10. The <object> and <embed> tags serve similar purposes for adding non-standard content to an HTML document. Compare these two tags and identify whether both are needed. Justify your position.

JavaScript and jQuery

This chapter introduces you to JavaScript, a language that can be used to enhance your Web sites with dynamic content. As part of this chapter, you will learn the basic tools of JavaScript and learn to use these tools to create form validation. You will also learn some of the common applications of JavaScript and some of the effects it can produce. This chapter also includes an introduction and overview of jQuery, a library for more easily creating complex effects in JavaScript across browsers. Once you have completed this chapter, you should be able to:

- Learn the variable declarations and syntax structures used in creating JavaScript scripts

- Use common functions in JavaScript to create dynamic effects on a page

- Incorporate JavaScript events into pages to invoke scripting based on user actions

- Install and use jQuery in a Web site application

6.1 JAVASCRIPT BASICS

JavaScript is a *scripting language* that can be embedded into HTML pages to enhance their functionality. Unlike HTML, Java-

Script does not establish the structure of a document but modifies elements of it based on the use of variables and functions like those used in traditional *programming languages*. Functionally, there is not a significant difference in the syntax of the languages; instead, the difference is in how each of them behaves. JavaScript is a *client-side language*, meaning all of the computations are done and actions are taken on the client's Web browser.

A **programming language** is a formal set of commands that can be used to manipulate data in a system; the programs using this kind of language are compiled and linked, turning the manually typed code into machine code prior to execution.

A **scripting language** is a formal set of commands that can be used to manipulate data in a system; the scripts using this kind of language are written without the steps to compile and link them into machine code prior to execution.

A client-side language, or front-end language, is a scripting or programming language that is executed on the local machine without involvement from the server. The client can view all source code.

A **server-side language**, or back-end language, is a scripting or programming language that is executed on the server, where only the results of the computation are delivered to the client machine. In general, the client does not see the source code.

Computational complexity is an estimate of how long it will take a program or a script to complete its operation. Syntax structures like loops and complex mathematics increase the complexity of a program or script. This can be measured in different units and is often a general estimate.

A **variable** is a named placeholder representing a data value that may or may not change during execution.

When JavaScript is invoked, the browser is using the computing resources of the local machine to process the information and compute the results. This means the server is not slowed down by this computation, but it also means the speed and efficiency of the script are determined by the state of the user's machine, which is generally unknown. For this reason, JavaScript works best when it is concise and limited in *computational complexity*.

The client-side nature of JavaScript means that any computations done in JavaScript cannot be guaranteed, because JavaScript is part of the client's machine; this is particularly important when considering the security of information sent from JavaScript to the server. There are languages that can process information passed back from the client browser and even pre-process information before it is sent to the client. These are *server-side languages*, and they will be the focus of the remaining two chapters of this text.

JavaScript can be invoked within an HTML page by using the *<script>* and *</script>* tags. These can be placed within the head or the body of the page. You can see an example of the use of these tags in the following code:

```
<html>
    <head>
    <script type="text/javascript">

    </script>
    ...
    </head>
    <body>
    ...
    </body>
    </html>
```

The *type* attribute is optional in HTML5, but it is required in HTML4. It is still a best practice to include it for browsers that are not fully compliant with the HTML5 standards yet. There is also a set of *<noscript>* and *</noscript>* tags for browsers that do not support JavaScript; any content placed within these tags will be displayed only when JavaScript is disabled or is not supported. All of the major modern browsers (even mobile browsers) fully support JavaScript, so the use of this tag is optional and typically unnecessary. An example of the use of the <noscript> tags follows:

```
<html>
   <head>
   <script type="text/javascript">

   </script>
   <noscript>Your browser does not support ↵
JavaScript, so the content of this page may not ↵
display as expected on your system.</noscript>
   ...
   </head>
   <body>
   ...
   </body>
   </html>
```

6.1.1 Variable Declarations

A *variable* is a named placeholder representing a data value that may or may not change during execution. It allows you to reference the name of the variable instead of hard-coding the data value itself. These are fundamental building blocks of all scripting and programming languages, and JavaScript is no exception to this. Unlike most languages, JavaScript uses the same variable declaration, *var*, for all types of data. This means you do not have to decide ahead of time what data type your variable will hold.

JavaScript is case sensitive, so the variable names jeeves, Jeeves, JeeVes, and jeeVes are all considered different variables in JavaScript. This means that you must watch your capitalization carefully and that you should review the naming of your variables if any of your scripts do not work as expected.

JavaScript variable names can contain any alphanumeric (alphabetic or numeric) characters and the underscore (_). Variable names cannot start with a number, so *3brooms* is an invalid variable name in JavaScript but *br00ms* is valid. To declare a variable in JavaScript, use the *var* declaration and the name of the variable, and end the line with a semicolon (;). An example of this for defining variables *x* and *y* is:

```
<script type="text/javascript">
    var x;
    var y;
</script>
```

Alternatively, you can combine these declarations into a single line by separating the variable names with a comma:

```
<script type="text/javascript">
    var x, y;
</script>
```

6.1.2 Assigning Values

When you initially declare a variable in JavaScript, it has the value *undefined*. This means that no computations can be performed on the variable, or the results will also have the value *undefined*. To assign an actual value to a variable, you use the equals sign (=) followed by the value you wish to store. There are a variety of data types that can be stored in a JavaScript variable. The most common ones include the following:

- *Boolean values:* These are *true* and *false*, which are most commonly used for evaluating conditional statements. These are reserved words (words that are part of the language itself) in JavaScript, so they can be typed as values without annotation.

- *Integer and decimal values:* These are numeric values that may or may not have a decimal component after them. Literal values do not require annotation and can be typed directly as a stored value.

- *Characters:* Each of these is a single symbol from the alphabet, the digits 0 through 9, or punctuation. A character must be wrapped in quotation marks (such as 'a'); by convention, characters use single quotation marks and strings use double quotation marks, but either is valid syntax in JavaScript.

- *Strings:* These are combinations of characters stored as a single value. A string must be wrapped in quotation marks (such as "Hello, World!"). By convention, strings are wrapped in double quotation marks, but both double and single quotation marks are valid syntax in JavaScript.

You can use comments in JavaScript to annotate code. A single-line comment in JavaScript is denoted by //, which tells the browser to ignore the rest of the line. Alternatively, using /* starts a multiline comment that ends only with a corresponding */. An example of the syntax for these comments follows:

```
<script type="text/javascript">
    var x, y; //This part is now a comment and ↵
will not be parsed as code.
    /* Everything within these symbols will be ↵
ignored as a comment, even across multiple lines ↵
of code. This is useful for debugging. */
</script>
```

An example of these declarations in code along with explanatory comments follows:

```
<script type="text/javascript">
    var x = true; // This is a Boolean value
    var y = 12.347; // This is a numeric assignment
    var c = 'A'; // This is a character assignment
    var s = "Hello, World!"; // This is a string as-
signment
</script>
```

When declaring variables, you can make multiple assignments in the same line. A variable can be referenced by its name; it can be reassigned at any time using the equals sign (=) syntax used to assign it initially. When a variable is referenced to give it a new assigned value, it must have its own line. An example of assigning multiple values in the same line is:

```
<script type="text/javascript">
    var x = true, y = 12.347, c = 'A', s = "Hello ↵
World!";
    y = 14; // This is a reassignment of value and ↵
must stand alone.
</script>
```

In addition to static values, variables can be assigned the results of mathematics, string concatenation, or even returned values from function calls (explained in the next section). Mathematical operations can be typed using the common format for the standard operations, along with parentheses and a minus sign (–) for negative values. String concatenation is accomplished by using the plus sign (+) between any two strings you wish to join (whether they are variables or literal values). Variables can be assigned the return value of a function only if the function actually returns a value. Examples of this type of assignment are shown in the following code:

```
<script type="text/javascript">
    var x = 2.3, y = 12.347, s1 = "Hello", s2 = ↵
"World!";

    x = (x*4)/3 + y - 1;
        s1 = s1 + "" + s2;
</script>
```

6.1.3 Function Calls

A *function* is a reusable set of lines of code that perform a specific task. It can take input through the use of parameters and return a single value. Functions are incredibly useful in code, because they allow you to reuse what you have already constructed. A collection of predefined functions is called a *library*. JavaScript has a large number of predefined functions available for use, such as the *alert()* function, which is covered in greater depth in section 6.2.1.

To call (or invoke) a function in JavaScript, you type the name of the function (which must be defined in code prior to the function call), followed by a left parenthesis, the arguments you wish to use according to the function's definition, a right parenthesis, and a semicolon. The *alert()* function, for instance, has one *parameter,* which accepts the text you wish to display as an alert. When you invoke the function and assign a specific value to the parameter, the value is called an *argument.* You can use literal values or variables as arguments when you invoke a function in JavaScript. Parameters appear in function definitions, and arguments appear in function calls. Function definitions are covered in section 6.1.4.

A **function** is a reusable set of lines of code that perform a specific task. It can take input through the use of parameters and return a single value.

A **library** is a collection of predefined functions that can be called in the code as soon as the library is attached to the page.

A **parameter** is a placeholder for an input value for a function that is defined when the function is written to determine how the function should behave.

An **argument** is a specific input value for a function when it is invoked for operation. The argument should be the same data type required by the parameter of the function it is filling.

The *alert()* function does not return a value, so you can call it without storing the result in another variable. An example of using the *alert()* function in JavaScript follows:

```
<script type="text/javascript">
    alert("Hello, World!");
</script>
```

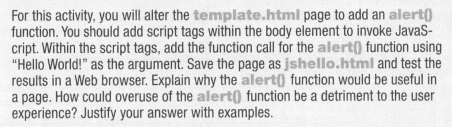

6.1.4 Defining Functions

JavaScript allows you to define your own functions as well. To
define a function, you need to know what parameters it should accept,
what it should accomplish, and what value (if any) it should return.
The rules for naming functions are the same rules that apply to naming variables. Due to the nature of variables in JavaScript, you can
simply name the parameters rather than specify the data type. If a
function needs to return a value, you should add a *return* statement
to the end of the function. An example of a trivial function follows, to
demonstrate the syntax:

```
<script type="text/javascript">
functionmessage_me(param) {
        alert(param);
        return true;
    }
</script>
```

In this example, the function name is *message_me* and the parameter is *param*. The function treats whatever text is used as an argument for *param* as an alert and returns the literal value *true*. When
the function is called, the argument given will take the place of *param*
in the content of the function. The lines of code included in the function are surrounded by curly braces ({ and }) to group them into the
definition of the function, as shown in the example.

To call this function, you need to do something with the returned value. You can set it to a new variable or assign the result to an existing variable. For trivial functions, it is better not to return anything, since the value is meaningless; the return statement is included here only for clarity of syntax. An example of the function definition and call for the *message_me()* function is:

```
<script type="text/javascript">
functionmessage_me(param)  {
          alert(param);
          return true;

}


     var x = "Hello, World!", y = false;
     y = message_me(x);
</script>
```

The function invocation here is alerting the contents of the variable *x* (which in this case is the string *Hello, World!*) and storing the return value (*true*) in the *y* variable.

The **scope** of a variable is an important consideration in function use. This is the part of the script or program where the variable is defined. You can define variables within a function, but they will be usable only within the function itself. Any changes you make to the value of the argument within a function will not change the original variable used as input. To change this variable, you have to call the variables defined outside of the function with an assignment (=) command inside the function itself. The following code has been annotated to clarify some of the issues surrounding scope:

```
<script type="text/javascript">
var x = "Hello, World!", y = false, c = 'A';

function message_me2(param)  {
          alert(param);
          var d = false; // This variable exists ⏎
```

```
⏎ only inside the function
param = "Goodbye"; /* This changes the value ⏎
only within the function */
c = 'B'; // This updates the external variable c
  }

    var x = "Hello, World!", y = false;
    message_me2(x); /* This function call will ⏎
change  the value of c to 'B,' but it will not ⏎
affect the value of x, which was used as an ⏎
argument. The variable d cannot be used outside ⏎
of the function, because it exists only while the ⏎
function is active. */
</script>
```

6.1.5 Conditional Statements

Conditional statements are a way to branch the execution of your script based on values of variables or object states. There are two primary statements used for conditional branching: *if* and *switch*. If statements evaluate a condition to see if it is true in order to execute its set of commands. A *switch* is a conditional branch that compares a value to preset results to determine which path to execute.

An *if* statement evaluates its argument to see if it is true or false. The argument can be any variable that contains a value of *true* or *false*, a conditional expression, or a combination of values that logically evaluates to *true* or *false*. The basic structure of an *if* statement in JavaScript is:

```
if (condition) {
    // These are statements that will execute only if
    condition is true
}
```

For conditional expressions, the following symbols can be used to evaluate comparisons of variables, functions, and literal values:

- $>$ will evaluate to true if the left side of the statement is greater than the right side; an example of this is $(x > y)$

- $>=$ will evaluate to true if the left side of the statement is greater than or equal to the right side ; an example of this is $(x >= y)$

- $<$ will evaluate to true if the left side of the statement is less than the right side; an example of this is $(x < y)$

- $<=$ will evaluate to true if the left side of the statement is less than or equal to the right side; an example of this is $(x <= y)$

- $==$ will evaluate to true only if both sides of the statement are equal; an example of this is $(x == y)$

- $!=$ will evaluate to true only if both sides of the statement are not equal; an example of this is $(x != y)$

Multiple values can be concatenated with logical operations for the conditional statement as well:

- $||$ represents an *OR* condition, which evaluates to true if either side of the statement is true; an example of this is (x || y)

- $\&\&$ represents an *AND* condition, which evaluates to true only if both sides of the statement are true; an example of this is (x && y)

Care must be taken to group chains of these statements correctly so that no more than two arguments are present for each of the concatenated elements. A statement can also be inverted using the *NOT* operator, which is represented by an exclamation point before the value; an example of this is $!(x)$ which would switch the boolean value of x. These elements can be combined into complex conditional evaluations, such as:

```
(((x > y))&&(y >= z))
```

An *if* statement can be extended to include an *else* case, which will execute if the condition evaluates to false. The structure for this is:

```
if (condition) {
```

```
    // These are statements that will execute only ↵
if the condition is true
} else {
    // These are statements that will execute only ↵
if the condition is false
}
```

An additional *if* statement can be added after the *else* to further branch the statement, as in the following:

```
if (condition1) {
    // These are statements that will execute only ↵
if condition1 is true
} else if (condition2) {
    /* These are statements that will execute only ↵
if condition1 is false and condition2 is true */
} else {
    /* These are statements that will execute only ↵
if condition1 and condition2 are false */
}
```

These *if* statements can also be nested, but care must be taken to make sure they are grouped correctly using the curly braces.

The *switch* statement evaluates a variable and compares it to defined cases. The *switch* statement typically operates on integers and characters. Each *case* will have its own set of statements. The *break* statement must be used at the end of a case to stop operation, or it will continue executing into the next case. A final *default* statement should be included to catch any exceptions, in which none of the cases matches the variable. The structure of a switch statement is:

```
switch (variable) {
    case 'A': // Note that the case is a literal value
        // This will execute if the variable == 'A'
        break; // This stops execution from moving
to the next case
    case 'B':
```

```
        // This will execute if the variable == 'B'
        break; // This stops execution from moving
    to the next case default:
        // This will execute if no other case
    matches the variable
        break; // This is not necessary, but it is
    good coding practice
    }
```

6.1.6 Looping

Looping is a repeated execution of the same set of statements. This is incredibly helpful if an action needs to be repeated or if a similar action needs to be performed repeatedly (such as counting from 1 to 5). There are three different basic types of loops that can be used in JavaScript: *for, while,* and *do/while.* Each of these will continue to operate while a condition is still valid.

 It is possible to create loops that do not ever stop. This happens if the condition for execution never becomes false; these are called **infinite loops**, and they will crash the user's browser. You must always make sure the loops you create will terminate.

A *for* loop has three statements as part of its signature: a statement that executes before the loop begins, a statement (condition) that determines whether the loop will execute, and a statement that executes after the loop finishes. An example showing the structure of a *for* loop is:

```
for (var x = 0; x < 5; x = x + 1) {
    // These are statements that will execute when
    the condition is true
    alert(x + 1);
}
```

In this example, the statement *var x = 0* executes before the loop ever starts. If $x < 5$, then the code of the loop, *alert(x + 1)*, executes. After the loop statements finish executing, the statement $x = x + 1$ will run. If the condition $x < 5$ is still true, the loop will run again; if not, the loop will stop and move to the next statement in the script.

There is also a for/in loop for working with arrays of data, but that is beyond the scope of this text and represents one of the more advanced functionalities of the JavaScript language.

A *while* loop has a simpler structure than a *for* loop. One thing to remember when using a *while* loop is to make sure the condition is eventually updated to become false; this will prevent it from being an infinite loop. An example of a *while* loop demonstrating such a structure is:

```
var x = 0;
while (x < 5) {
    // These are statements that will execute when
the condition is true
    alert(x + 1);
    x = x + 1; // This is the statement to update the
condition
}
```

In this instance, the operation is the same as that in the *for* loop outlined in the previous example. You should note where the statements have been placed in the *while* loop. The only requirement for the *while* loop is having a conditional statement to evaluate. The last statement of the code block is there to make sure the *while* loop will terminate, as well as setting the increment for the count. Most *for* and *while* loops can be written interchangeably, but care must be taken to make sure the operation is correct when converting between them.

A *do/while* loop has a structure similar to that of a *while* loop, but it forces execution of the loop once before testing the condition at all. An example of a *do/while* loop showing the syntax is:

```
var x = 0;
do {
   /* These are statements that will execute once
and will repeat if the condition is true */
   alert(x + 1);
   x = x + 1; // This is the statement to update the
condition
} while (x < 5); // This will determine the condi-
tion for continuation
```

Loop statements can also be nested to perform more complex computations and functions. Loops are incredibly useful and very adaptable tools for coding in any language.

ACTIVITY 6.2 – COUNTING BOT

ACTIVITY

For this activity, you will create a page from the template.html page to use JavaScript to alert the numbers from 0 to 10. Within the script tags, add a loop to alert the numbers from 0 to 10 and then stop. Save the page as count_bot.html and test the results in a Web browser. Explain the loop you constructed and the parameters that were needed to make it function correctly.

6.2 USING JAVASCRIPT

JavaScript is a rich and complex language. Learning its full scope would take much more than just a chapter. However, there are a number of common functions and applications of JavaScript that will give you the initial practice you need to get started with adding this powerful and dynamic content to your Web pages. This part of the chapter focuses on some of the most common applications of JavaScript, which you can use and modify for your own pages.

6.2.1 Using the *alert()* Function

Now that you have some practice with using the *alert()* function, you can consider its practical applications in a page. The primary purpose of the *alert()* function is to notify users of some piece of information. Originally, this would be used to alert users to errors in their form data or problems with page execution. Dynamic content changes the page itself and lets users know inside the page if there is an error, providing a better user experience. This is what you will do for the case project contact form. The *alert()* function still has a significant use, though. You can use it to display internal variables when you need to debug a page. When an alert is triggered, it will pause the execution until the pop-up window created by the alert is closed, so you can freeze your script at that point and see what value is stored in a variable that is not behaving as expected. An example of this type of use is:

```
<script type="text/javascript">
var x = 24, y = 12;

x = x*2 + y;
alert(x); // This will display the current value of x
x = x/3;
alert(x); // This will display the new value of x
</script>
```

It is important to remember to comment out or delete the *alert()* functions used to debug your code prior to posting it live on your site.

6.2.2 String Parsing and Form Validation

One of the most useful applications of JavaScript since its inception is to provide client-side form validation (making sure the user-entered data in the form is correct). JavaScript has a library of functions for use in parsing and comparing strings. These will be explored to construct a form validation script for the case project. This will make sure that each field in the contact form is completed correctly before it is submitted to the destination identified in the *action* attribute of the form.

There are several fields that need to be completed and some that have data considerations, particularly the e-mail address for the user. To begin, a function should be constructed to process the form data before sending it to the back-end server (for repeat processing). Everything in JavaScript is an object within a hierarchy on the page, so this structure will be used to identify each piece of the form that will be validated. This structure can take time to understand, so try to follow each example closely and understand how the references work before moving to the next. The JavaScript that will provide the form validation framework is:

```
<!DOCTYPE html>
<html>
    <head>
    ...

<script type="text/javascript">
    Function validateContact() {
        // This will be the function body
        return true;
    }
</script>
</head>
<body>
    ...
```

```
<form name="contact" action="contact.php" ↵
onsubmit="return validateContact();"method="POST">
    ...
</body>
</html>
```

In the code above, the function *validateContact()* is given a blank framework, while the event *onsubmit* is attached to the form itself. If the form validation fails, this function needs to return a false value so the form submission does not complete. If the default behavior is set to return false, then the form will never submit. You can test this in a browser to verify the results.

The first item that will be checked is that the *myname* text box contains at least some text. JavaScript contains a *length* property as part of the string class that returns the length of a string. This can be done with the following code:

```
function validateContact() {
    if (document.contact.myname.value.length <= 0) {
        alert("The name field cannot be empty.");
        return false;
    }
return true;
}
```

Note the reference to the form object *contact* and the *myname* field within the form. The *value* property refers to the text within the field itself. Any of the fields in a form can be referenced by this sequence, in which the name of the field is substituted for *myname* in the example. This same test can be applied to the *e-mail* and *message* fields as follows:

```
function validateContact() {
    if (document.contact.myname.value.length<= 0) {
        alert("The name field cannot be empty.");
        return false;
    }
```

```
        if (document.contact.email.value.length<= 0) {
                alert("The email field cannot be empty.");
                return false;
        }
        if (document.contact.message.value.length<= 0) {
                alert("The message field cannot be
empty.");
                return false;
        }
return true;
        }
```

Note that each of these fields must be evaluated separately, so each one requires a separate *if* statement to evaluate the length for a potential problem. The issue with the code above is that once there is a failure in the validation, it ends and returns false. It is better to let the user know what all of the problems are with the form at once rather than force them to resubmit for each one, so the false value will be determined by a new variable called *okay,* which is initially set to *true* (so the form will be submitted) and then set to *false* if there is a problem. You can see this new code in action below:

```
function validateContact() {
    var okay = true;
if (document.contact.myname.value.length<= 0) {
        alert("The name field cannot be empty.");
        okay = false;
    }
    if (document.contact.email.value.length<= 0) {
        alert("The email field cannot be empty.");
        okay = false;
    }
    if (document.contact.message.value.length<= 0) {
        alert("The message field cannot be empty.");
```

```
        okay = false;
    }

returnokay;

}
```

This function will now check the entire form before returning a result.

Returning to the validation of the *myname* field, names generally do not have numbers, so you could specify that they are to be excluded. Several characters, though, must be excluded for the safety of the back-end system where this form will be processed. These are quotation marks (' and "), the semicolon (;), the ampersand (&), and the escape character (\ ); all are risky to allow, since they could corrupt data or be used to initiate an attack on the server. To make sure the name does not contain these unsafe characters, you can invoke the JavaScript *test()* function for parsing strings.

This takes a *regular expression* as an object, which is a formalized way to express a group of characters. The syntax of regular expressions can become very complex, so this example will group the unwanted characters in a single expression, which is commonly denoted in JavaScript with the format */expression/g*. The pipe character (|) is used to separate characters in the list, representing an *OR* condition.

The escape character (\) has to be used in strings and regular expressions when you want to use a literal character in place of one that would otherwise terminate the string or expression. For instance, to add a double quotation mark within a string, you have to escape the double quotation mark as follows: "This string contains a \" mark" to make it a valid string in JavaScript. Whenever you want to reference the escape character itself as a literal value, you have to escape the escape character as follows: \\.

The code to perform the validation test described on the content of *myname* is:

```
function validateContact() {
    var okay = true;

    ...

    var pattern = /;|'|"|&|\\/g;
    if (pattern.test(document.contact.myname.value))
{
        alert("The name field contains invalid ↵
characters. These include & ; ` \" and \\.");
        okay = false;
    }
returnokay;
}
```

Note the use of the *escape* character in both the regular expression and the string that is being used as the argument for the alert. The *test()* function works only on regular expression objects like the one defined for the *pattern* variable. Once again, this same test should be applied to the *e-mail* and *message* fields as well.

While these tests are sufficient for the *myname* and *message* fields, some additional tests need to be performed on the *e-mail* field to make sure it at least has the necessary structure of an e-mail address. It is almost impossible to truly validate an e-mail address, but the two characteristics it must have are a single @ character and at least one period after the @ with at least two characters after it. This test will be performed to make sure the e-mail address fits the basic structure, though the address may still be invalid.

To test for specific characters in an e-mail address or any string, there are two methods within the string object that can be used: *indexOf()* and *lastIndexOf()*. Both of these accept characters as arguments and will return an integer value indicating where in the string the character occurs. If the value returned is *-1*, then the character is not located within the string. Note that the first character in a string in JavaScript is counted at position 0. The code to perform these tests is:

```
function validateContact() {
    var okay = true;
...
    varat_position = document.contact.email.value.in-
    dexOf('@');
    vardot_position = document.contact.email.value. ↵
    lastIndexOf('.');
    varemail_length = document.contact.email.value. ↵
    length;
    if (((at_position< 1)||(dot_position< 1))||((dot_ ↵
    position + 2) > email_length)) {
        alert("The email address entered is not valid.");
            okay = false;
    }
    return okay;
}
```

The code will find the position of the @ symbol, the last period in the e-mail address, and the length of the e-mail address. The conditional evaluation will make sure both the @ and the period are present and then make sure there are at least two characters after the period. This is a minimal check of an e-mail address; there are many more ways to test this value, but they can become exhaustive and cumbersome, when the biggest risk of an invalid e-mail address is undeliverable mail. For businesses, it is wise to include a second field to have the user verify the address by entering it a second time. This will minimize typos and mistakes.

The last step to be performed in this validation is to make sure one of the radio buttons is selected for the preferred method of contact. If you look at the code, you will see that the form field name is the same for both options. It must be the same for the options to work as a group. In order to test which one is selected, you need to add an identifier that can be used to select them individually; the value of the field will not work for this purpose. You should be familiar with using *ID* values in tags now, so you can add the following code to create an ID for each radio box:

```
*** INSERT CODE
<form name="contact" action="contact.php"
onsubmit="return validateContact();" method="POST">
    ...
<input type="radio" name="preference" id="pref_ ↵
email" value="Email">Email<br />
    <input type="radio" name="preference" id="pref_ ↵
phone" value="Phone">Phone<br />
    ...
</form>
```

You can now use JavaScript to test whether either of these is selected. The method to find a tag by its ID value is *getElementById()*. This accepts a string value as an argument to reference the ID inside the tag. The method for testing whether a radio button is selected is called *checked*. The code to test whether either of the options is selected is:

```
function validateContact() {
    var okay = true;
    ...
if (!document.getElementById("pref_email").checked ↵
&& !document.getElementById("pref_phone").checked) {
    alert("A preferred method of contact must be ↵
selected.");
    okay = false;
}
return okay;
}
```

This code will generate an error if both "E-mail" and "Phone" remain unselected. This is accomplished by inverting the result of the *checked* method and combining both statements with an *AND* operator.

There are a number of other useful functions for validating various types of form input, but this will get you started with validating your own form data. In the next section, you will learn how to make the messages to the user more user-friendly and make your Web site look more professional.

6.2.3 Dynamic Content

One of the more popular uses of JavaScript is to dynamically rewrite page content without reloading a page for the user. This can be used to provide feedback on forms or to display and hide elements of the page. This works particularly well in conjunction with CSS. The application of this dynamic content that will be explored in this section is to provide feedback on the form errors on the page itself rather than to generate *alert* boxes. To do this, new structural elements need to be added to the form so that the *alert* information has a place to go. The <div> tag will perform this function, as seen in the following code:

```
<form name="contact" action="contact.php"
onsubmit="return validateContact();" method="POST">
    <div id="name_err"></div>
    Name:
    <select name="salutation">
        ...
    </select>
    <input type="text" name="myname"><br />
    <div id="email_err"></div>
    Email: <input type="text" name="email"><br />
    <div id="method_err"></div>
    Preferred Method of Contact: <br/>
    <input type="radio" name="preference" id="pref_ ↵
email" value="Email">Email<br />
    <input type="radio" name="preference" id="pref_ ↵
phone" value="Phone">Phone<br />
```

```
<input type="checkbox" name="subscribe" ↵
value="Yes"> Subscribe to the Zippy Beans ↵
newsletter!<br />
    <div id="message_err"></div>
    Message:<br/>
    <textarea name="message" rows="4" cols="50"> ↵
</textarea> <br/>
    <input type="submit" value="Submit!">
</form>
```

You can test this in a browser to see that the empty <div>tags do not change the display at all. You can add style classes to these elements so they are displayed in red text to alert the user to the content.

The means to access the contents of an HTML tag as a JavaScript object within a page is called *innerHTML*. This value can be retrieved as a string or set to a new string value. An example of this for the first error in the name value is:

```
function validateContact() {

    ...

if (document.contact.myname.value.length <= 0) {
        document.getElementById("name_err"). ↵
innerHTML = "The name field cannot be empty.";
        okay = false;
    }

    ...

    }
```

Try to submit the form with an empty *name* value to see this effect in action. All of the remaining alerts will still generate pop-ups, but the name length error will show up in the page.

Adding this code to each of the errors would be cumbersome, so it will be easier to create a new function that will perform this task. You can then reference the function for each of the errors generated. A sample function to perform this task is:

```
functionerrDisplay(elementID,message) {
```

```
      document.getElementById(elementID).innerHTML = ↵
message;
   }


   functionvalidateContact() {
   ...
   }
```

You can now replace the alerts with calls to the new function, such as:

```
function validateContact() {
      ...
   if (document.contact.myname.value.length<= 0) {
            errDisplay("name_err","The name field ↵
cannot be empty.");
            okay = false;
      }
   ...
   }
```

The final step is to clear the error values whenever the form is submitted. This can be accomplished using the same function already defined:

```
function validateContact() {
      var okay = true;
   errDisplay("name_err","");
      errDisplay("email_err","");
      errDisplay("method_err","");
      errDisplay("message_err","");
   ...
   }
```

You can see an example of this functionality in Figure 6.1.

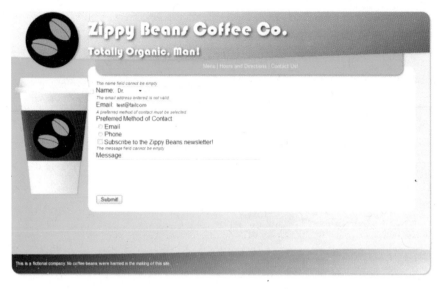

▲ **FIGURE 6.1** Sample Functionality of Dynamic Form Content

This is just one example of using dynamic content. It can be applied to show tooltips or hints, or even to personalize pages. It is a versatile tool for generating engaging and dynamic user experiences on a Web site.

6.2.4 Events

An *event* in JavaScript is generated whenever a user takes an action on a page. These events can be captured within various tags, such as images and links, to detect things like the mouse clicking a tag element or the mouse moving within a tag. These are attached to the tag as attributes, just like an ID or a source. The value of these attributes is a line of code that can be executed as JavaScript. This code can call functions, make assignments, or perform any task that JavaScript can accomplish.

You may have noticed in the contact form that the user has the option to select "Phone" as a preferred method of contact but that there is no place to enter a phone number. JavaScript will be used to create this box dynamically when the "Phone" option is selected. This will be done using a custom function, *innerHTML*, and the *onchange* event attribute.

The function will have to test whether the *phone* field is displayed or not and then toggle the display accordingly. The code for this is:

```
function phoneDisplay() {
    if (document.getElementById("pref_phone").
checked) {
        document.getElementById("phone_div"). ↵
innerHTML = "Phone Number: <input type=\"text\" ↵
name=\"phone\">";
    } else {
        document.getElementById("phone_div"). ↵
innerHTML = "";
    }
}
```

The structural code to support this is the addition of a <div> tag with the ID *phone_div* to hold the content. In the form, this will be:

```
*** INSERT CODE
<form name="contact" action="contact. ↵
php" onsubmit="return validateContact();" ↵
method="POST">
    ...
    <input type="radio" name="preference" ↵
id="pref_phone" value="Phone">Phone<br />
    <div id="phone_div"></div>
<input type="checkbox" name="subscribe" ↵
value="Yes">Subscribe to the Zippy Beans
newsletter!<br />
    ...

</form>
```

Finally, the *event* code that will call the function whenever the radio button selection is changed is:

```
<form name="contact" action="contact. ↵
php" onsubmit="return validateContact();"
```

```
method="POST">

    …

    <input type="radio" name="preference" id="pref_
↵email" onchange="phoneDisplay()"value="Email">Email
↵<br />
<input type="radio" name="preference" id="pref_ ↵
phone" onchange="phoneDisplay()"value="Phone"> ↵
Phone<br />

    …

</form>
```

This is just one example of an event in JavaScript. These can be added to almost any tag that allows user interaction and can be coded to react to the user's exploration of the page.

ACTIVITY 6.3 – VALIDATING THE PHONE NUMBER

For this activity, you will add another piece of verification to the form in contact.html. With the addition of the script to dynamically generate the phone field, you should add verification to make sure the phone number is valid. It should have at least ten digits and should not contain any letters. Be sure to test in the code whether the phone number should be included (if phone is chosen as the preferred contact method) so it does not test a value that does not exist when you attempt to submit the form. What strategy did you use to perform these tests in JavaScript? Explain your answer.

6.2.5 External JavaScript

Just as with CSS, you can create an external file to store your JavaScript code and link it to your page. This is particularly useful for functions you define that apply to multiple pages within your site. The common extension for a JavaScript file is *.js*.

If you have a set of functions that applies to your entire site, you should name your file *main.js*. If it applies to a specific page (such as a contact page), you can call the set by the name of the page (such as *contact.js*), for clarity. You should move function definitions only to an external JavaScript file, because whenever the file is attached to the page, the contents of the file will execute. If you have code that applies to a specific part of the page, it should be left where it is.

To create an external JavaScript file, copy everything you want to move externally to a blank text document and save it with the *.js* extension. That file should not contain any script tags at all, since it is not HTML content. In the HTML page, you will modify the script tag to include a source attribute, such as:

```
<script src="include/contact.js" type="text/javas-
cript"></script>
```

The path to the external JavaScript file should be relative to the location of the page itself, just as it was for the external CSS document. Whenever a script tag has a *source* attribute, it must not contain any additional scripting. You must create a new script tag set to insert additional script content. You can see an example of this here:

```
<script src="include/contact.js" type"text/javas-
cript"></script>
<script type="text/javascript">
// Additional script commands can be placed here.
</script>
```

ACTIVITY 6.4 – EXTERNAL JAVASCRIPT

For this activity, you will create an external JavaScript file for the contact page of the case project. You should save the external JavaScript file as contact.js. Briefly describe what JavaScript content was moved out of the HTML page and what was left in the page. What are the benefits of using external files for JavaScript? Is it important to use external JavaScript for a single page in the site, as in the example here? Justify your answer.

6.3 JQUERY

As it has developed, JavaScript has been modified with functionality that applies only to specific browsers. A notable example of this is separate functionality on Internet Explorer and Mozilla Firefox.

While this is not part of the core functionality of JavaScript, it can be used to provide significant enhancements to a user's experience. It can be used for effects such as repositioning elements on the screen or creating dynamic tooltips. To get around the browser differences and take advantage of this functionality, developers have to write code that identifies the browser and then operates based on the specific browser's format.

Libraries have been developed to simplify this type of coding across browsers and generally make it easier for developers to use the more advanced features of JavaScript. One of the most popular and comprehensive of these libraries is jQuery, which is available for free download at *http://jquery.com*. This library allows you to create dynamic pop-ups, add drag-and-drop functionality, and perform a myriad of other tasks with simplified coding. The remainder of this chapter will provide a brief introduction to using jQuery, but this is an extensive library that, like JavaScript itself, would take more than one chapter to fully explore.

6.3.1 Installing jQuery

From the jQuery Web site (*jquery.com*), there are two options for the code you wish to download, *Development* and *Production*. The Development selection is the more straightforward, but it has a larger file size; this is uncompressed code that will be either displayed in the browser or downloaded to your machine. If the code is displayed in your browser, you can copy the page (use Select All if necessary) and save the results as *jquery.js*. If you download the file to your machine, you can rename the file *jquery.js* or use the original file name in your source path.

 The Production (compressed) file for the jQuery library has a different naming convention. The Development version is used in this chapter for clarity and simplicity. The Development version makes the jQuery library readable should you wish to explore how any of its functions work.

You can add this file to any of your Web projects by pasting a copy of this file wherever you store your other external JavaScript files. Inside any HTML page, you can link the jQuery library to your page the same way you use any other external JavaScript file. For example, if you had all of your external JavaScript (including *jquery.js*) in the *Include* folder, you would use the code:

```
<script src="include/jquery.js"></script>
```

This activates the jQuery library for use in your page. You can now use script tags (without the *type* attribute) to write jQuery code inside your page. For example, you could use the following script to generate an alert as soon as the document is ready to begin loading on the screen:

```
<script src="include/jquery.js"></script>
<script>
    $(document).ready(function(){
        alert("Hello, jQuery!");
    });
</script>
```

If you can get this code to work correctly in a page on your site, the jQuery library is installed and functional for that site. You can save this in a page called *jtest.html,* which can be reused from site to site to make sure jQuery is working before you begin scripting; just be sure to update the *src* path to the correct location of *jquery.js*.

6.3.2 jQuery Code and Use

While the example from Section 6.2.4 will work in practice for dynamically adding the text box for a phone number entry, it requires coding the HTML structure within the JavaScript, which is not a best practice. Using jQuery, you can accomplish the same task of showing and hiding the phone number entry while it is coded in the HTML structure itself. To begin, you will need to create two CSS classes either in the external style sheet or within the *contact.html* page. These involve the display style command:

```css
.myphone {
    display: none;
}
.show {
    display: block;
}
```

You also need to adjust the structure of the <div> tags that contain the phone number. This involves adding a class to hide the entry and adding the form field itself within the structure of the page. The code for this is:

```
*** INSERT CODE
<form …>

    …

Preferred Method of Contact: <br/>
    <input type="radio" name="preference" ↵
id="pref_email" onchange="phoneDisplay()" ↵
value="Email">Email<br />
    <input type="radio" name="preference" ↵
id="pref_phone" onchange="phoneDisplay()" ↵
value="Phone">Phone<br />
    <div id="phone_div" class="myphone">Phone ↵
Number: <input type=text name="phone"></div>
    <input type="checkbox" name="subscribe" ↵
value="Yes"> Subscribe to the Zippy Beans ↵
newsletter!<br />

    …

</form>
```

You also need to add the jQuery library to your *contact.html* page, using the instructions in the previous section. With this enabled, you can take advantage of the *addClass()* function in jQuery to dynamically adjust the CSS of an element within the page. The similar function *removeClass()* will take away a class from a tag. Both of these take a *string* argument that references a CSS class defined in the style sheets for the page; this can be an external or an internal style. By adding or removing the CSS class to reveal the display, you can change whether the element appears in the page display.

To invoke these functions, you can refer to an element by its tag and class using dot notation (such as *div.myphone*). The call to jQuery is signified by the dollar (*$*) sign. The code for toggling the display of the phone number value can then be updated to the following:

```
<script type="text/javascript">
functionphoneDisplay() {
    if (document.getElementById("pref_phone").
checked) {
        $("div.myphone").addClass("show"); ↵
/* This is the new jQuery code */
    } else {
        $("div.myphone").removeClass("show");
    }
}
...
</script>
```

jQuery has an extensive array of functionality, and this is just a small example. It is recommended that you learn both JavaScript basics and jQuery to make the most of this coding library. A working knowledge of CSS is also required to make these commands function effectively. The jQuery Web site has extensive tutorials and API documentation for you to learn the library and practice its applications.

CHAPTER SUMMARY

This chapter showcased JavaScript and its ability to create dynamic content within a page and alter the display of a single page based on user interaction. This is an incredibly powerful language that can be added seamlessly into HTML documents across all modern browsers, from desktops to mobile devices. The jQuery library was also introduced, with instructions for its inclusion in Web sites and its practical use. JavaScript is a client-side language, so all of the content created up to this point can be tested on a local browser. The remaining two chapters of this text focus on server-side languages, which require Web hosting in order to test and use them, since the server compiles the code before delivering the result to the client browser. The next chapter introduces you to two server-side scripting languages and gives a brief overview of Web hosting.

CHAPTER KNOWLEDGE CHECK

1 Which of the following is not allowed as part of a JavaScript variable name?

- ○ **A.** letters
- ○ **B.** numbers
- ○ **C.** the underscore character
- ○ **D.** the @ symbol
- ○ **E.** None of the above

2 Which of the following is not a type of loop in JavaScript?

- ○ **A.** *do*
- ○ **B.** *while*
- ○ **C.** *for*
- ○ **D.** *when*

3 A conditional *if* statement can operate on any variable or statement that evaluates to *true* or *false*.

   ○ **A.** True

   ○ **B.** False

4 Which of the following is a valid variable declaration in JavaScript?

   ○ **A.** var a; b

   ○ **B.** var a = This text;

   ○ **C.** var a = true

   ○ **D.** var a, b;

   ○ **E.** None of the above

5 Which of the following reserved words in JavaScript is not associated with coding a switch statement?

   ○ **A.** default

   ○ **B.** case

   ○ **C.** break

   ○ **D.** do

   ○ **E.** All of the above

   ○ **F.** None of the above

6 A function takes _____ when called in code.

   ○ **A.** Parameters

   ○ **B.** Arguments

   ○ **C.** Variables

   ○ **D.** Values

7 The type of data stored in a JavaScript variable does not have to be specified when the variable is declared.

   ○ **A.** True

   ○ **B.** False

8

jQuery is a separate programming language that interacts with JavaScript inside an HTML page.

- ○ **A.** True
- ○ **B.** False

9

A coding library is a _____.

- ○ **A.** complete syntax for a scripting or programming language.
- ○ **B.** method for defining an external file containing code.
- ○ **C.** collection of functions that can be reused in code.
- ○ **D.** All of the above
- ○ **E.** None of the above

10

A value can be assigned to a variable in JavaScript at the time it is defined.

- ○ **A.** True
- ○ **B.** False

CHAPTER PROJECTS

Project 1: Personal Web Site

For this project, you should create the validation for the contact page on your site. This should do a first pass on the data entered to make sure it is valid. Document your code with comments to explain the process of validation that is being performed. Be sure to add the structural elements to your HTML to allow reporting of any errors within the fields themselves.

Project 2: Resort Web-Site

For this project, you should build out a script that cycle through images on your home page to advertise the various accommodations and options. Each image should be displayed for a set amount of time and then change. The *onload* attribute within the <body> tag can call the function initially, and then it should update the picture through a loop. (You can also use *document.ready()* if you have jQuery installed on your page.) Be sure that the loop is designed to terminate. In the code documentation, explain how the function works.

CHAPTER EXERCISES

1. Describe the two formats for comments in JavaScript. Give two examples for cases in which each would be useful in code.

2. Define a loop in JavaScript to count from 0 to 20 by increments of 2. Explain the choice of loop and the parameters needed to make this work correctly.

3. Define a switch statement in JavaScript that switches on a numerical value from 1 to 12 and displays the month as an alert. The default case should alert the user that the value is not equal to a month. Explain how your statement works.

4. Explain the path name used to access a form field value within an HTML page in JavaScript. Use an example and define what each part of the path name represents.

5. Give at least two additional applications of using *innerHTML*. What kinds of effects can be created with this functionality?

6. Use the Web to research additional methods of parsing strings in JavaScript. Identify two functions that can be used for this purpose and give an example of how they could be used.

7. Use the Web to research additional events in JavaScript that can be used to initiate JavaScript code. Identify two events, explain when they would be activated, and make a short list of tags to which they could be added.

8. Can any *if-else* statement be converted to a *switch* statement in JavaScript? Can any *switch* statement be converted into an *if-else* statement? Give examples to explain your answer.

9. Give an example of string concatenation in JavaScript. What happens when you concatenate a numerical value to the string? Test this and explain your findings.

10. Using the documentation available on *www.jquery.com*, choose an additional piece of functionality that jQuery includes and explain how to use it in a simple example.

CHAPTER REVIEW QUESTIONS

1. Explain the difference between arguments and parameters in your own words. Define and call a simple function in JavaScript code to showcase the difference and justify your answer.

2. When would JavaScript be more beneficial within a page than external to the page? Give an example to justify your answer.

3. Briefly explain the benefits of coding libraries like jQuery. How do they make scripting and programming easier for a developer? Justify your answer.

4. Briefly explain the purpose of using an alert in debugging code. Why is the *alert()* function not considered user-friendly?

5. Briefly explain the difference between a programming language and a scripting language. Why is JavaScript considered a scripting language? Explain your answer.

6. Briefly explain the difference between a client-side language and a server-side language. What are the benefits of using each type of language? Justify your answer.

7. Are all of the different loop types in JavaScript interchangeable? Give examples to justify your answer.

8. In normal programming languages, why is it sometimes acceptable to use an infinite loop? What is the risk of using this in any language? Explain your answer.

9. Why must a function definition be added to a page prior to the function being called within a page? What does this mean for the order of defining a function used within another function? Explain your answer.

10. Explain why cross-browser functionality is an issue in JavaScript. You can use Internet Explorer and Mozilla Firefox as examples. How do libraries like jQuery help developers to overcome these problems? Explain your answer.

PHP and Perl

This chapter introduces you to the basic back-end, or server-side, languages PHP and Perl. Both of these languages are full-featured and capable of creating robust Web applications. Learning one of these languages (or a similar back-end language, like Java Server Pages (JSP) or Active Server Pages [ASP]) will allow you to develop a full Web site for yourself or for a client. Once you have completed this chapter, you should be able to:

- Understand the concept of Web hosting and know where to find a Web host for your site

- Produce dynamic content on a Web page from the server side

- Create a form-processing page in both PHP and Perl

- Use either PHP or Perl to send e-mail as part of a Web application

7.1 HOSTING A WEB SITE

Up to this point in the text, everything you have created can be tested on your local machine, but with the inclusion of *back-end lan-*

guages, you will need a live Web site for testing your code. In most cases, when you create a Web site, you will want it to be publicly accessible, so you will also need a domain name so people can find the site. There are two services you will need to create a fully operational Web site: domain name registration and Web hosting. Domain name registration is the reservation of a human-readable Web address (URL) and an association between that name and the server location where the HTML pages reside. Domain name registration can typically be done as part of Web hosting.

Back-end languages, also called **server-side languages**, are programming languages used within Web sites that are compiled on the server before the results are sent to the client's browser. The source code for back-end languages is typically hidden from the user. These languages are not limited on the host machine, like JavaScript, and can access the full functionality of the machine on which they reside, including e-mail services and the file structure within the folder or folders allocated for the domain.

Web hosting is a service that allows remote storage of files used on a Web site, which can be accessed through a domain name or an assigned IP address. The scope of access is determined by the owner of the site and the type of hosting being used. Having a Web site hosted on a server is necessary for connecting to a site from a remote client machine as well as for development tasks such as testing server-side languages and sending e-mail from within a Web application.

Web hosting is a service provided by companies like GoDaddy (*www.godaddy.com*), which offer you a share of server space for a monthly or annual fee. There are a lot of pieces that go into hosting your Web site. The most common issues to consider are:

- *Domain name registration:* The domain name is the URL of your Web site. It should contain a combination of characters that is easy to remember and relevant to the content of the site. This will be the human-language address of the site, such as *www.apple.com* or *www.microsoft.com*. You typically have to pay for a domain name with a domain name registrar. It is recommended that you use the same company to register your domain name that you use to host the domain; otherwise you will need to have additional configuration to get the name linked to the hosting server.

- *Domain Name Service (DNS) entries:* The Domain Name Service is a way to resolve the human-readable URL to an actual server IP address. Managing the data entries for linking the server to the domain name can be difficult, depending on the host and the domain registry; for this reason it is recommended that you purchase the domain name from the hosting provider when it is possible.

- *ICANN information:* The Internet Corporation for Assigned Names and Numbers (ICANN) is the organization that manages the global allocation of Internet Protocol version 4 (IPv4) and Internet Protocol version 6 (IPv6) address space, including any static address you will associate to your domain name that will reference the specific folder on the server where your Web site files will reside. ICANN operates the Internet Assigned Numbers Authority (IANA) on behalf of the United States government. This means that you must provide ICANN with valid and verifiable contact information for the ownership of any Web address housed within the United States; this information becomes part of the public record as part of the WHOIS database available at *whois.net*. Whenever you register a domain, you must provide this information before your domain name will be activated; most hosting services will guide you through this process either as part of domain name registration or as part of the Web hosting configuration.

- *Server space:* This is the amount of storage space you will be allowed for your Web site. The purpose and volume of your media will typically determine how much storage space you will need. The more media-centric or data-centric your site is, the more space you should reserve. More space will generally cost more money.

- *E-mail accounts:* Some hosting options provide you with e-mail accounts for your reserved domain name. You should consider the number of e-mail addresses you will need with the domain extension as part of your hosting decision. More e-mail accounts generally cost more money. For sites like the ones you are constructing in this text, a single e-mail account should be sufficient.

- *Traffic/bandwidth limitations:* This is the amount of traffic that your site will be allowed to use each month. This may be tracked in terms of concurrent connections to the site or overall volume of data downloaded. You should carefully review what happens if this limit is exceeded; this can cause the host to suspend your site (which is bad for viewers), slow down traffic to your site, or charge you for the overage incurred. The purpose and audience size for the site should determine this metric. You should also research your ability to change this bandwidth based on traffic patterns once your site is live; it is typically easier to increase bandwidth on a plan than it is to reduce it. Higher bandwidth often costs more money.

- *Languages supported:* This is the listing of server-side programming languages that are supported by the hosting option. For the purpose of this text, you should look for hosting options that support PHP and/or Perl as well as MySQL for data storage (which will be covered in the next chapter). There are other popular server-side languages, such as JSP, ASP, and Ruby on Rails, that you may wish to learn once you are familiar with the concepts of front-end and back-end programming on the Web.

There are a myriad of different Web sites that offer hosting solutions and services. Some of these sites are safe, and some of them will take your personal information to sell. You have to be very careful with what you give to any Web site, especially your credit card information. You should always look at customer reviews for the service before you share any information with the site. If you have to enter any information to get the prices or product information, you should generally avoid that site. Any reputable Web hosting service will offer its service details up front without requiring any information from you.

The author of this text has consistently used GoDaddy® (www.godaddy.com) as a hosting company for several years without any significant issues. Overall, it has been a reliable and cost-effective solution that supports most of the major languages used for programming on the Web. If you are looking for a hosting solution that is safe and reliable, the author recommends GoDaddy as a starting point.

Because of the volume of hosting options, there is no general guide to setting up your Web hosting, but a good Web host will provide details on how to load and manage your site once you have enrolled in their hosting program.

7.2 PHP

PHP is a recursive acronym that stands for Hypertext Preprocessor. Like that of Perl, though, the reality of this acronym is up for debate; the original author of the toolset that would become PHP, Rasmus Lerdorf, named his toolkit Personal Home Page Tools, or PHP Tools. PHP is one of the most common server-side languages in use today. It is a very powerful language, and it embeds easily into any HTML document. PHP documents can reside anywhere within a Web site and use the extension *.php*. When a server is configured with it, PHP will automatically process the page on the server before sending the result to the client machine when it encounters this file type. Hosting options that offer PHP typically require little to no configuration from the user before using PHP within the server pages.

Because server-side languages process their output before sending the results to the client machine, they are not interactive. The results of the code will be processed linearly and send to the client; any content changes or dynamic interaction on the page will require that the results be sent back to the server for it to re-process the results. Client-side languages like JavaScript can bridge the gap in interactivity and minimize the number of times the server must be invoked to produce new content.

7.2.1 PHP Basics

PHP code can be embedded directly into an HTML document, allowing you to establish the framework and structure of the page and to provide data processing and dynamic content. This is ideal if you are learning HTML and CSS for the first time, because it allows you to utilize what you already know and build an additional language into the structure. PHP is inserted as tags into a page, just like other HTML elements. The tags for PHP are *<?php* to open the PHP code and *?>* to close the PHP code. Any text that exists between these tags will be treated as code.

PHP must be installed on the server in order for PHP pages to compile. If it is not installed, the source code itself will be displayed without processing on most browsers, which will treat the PHP tag indicators as unknown tags; other browsers will produce an error. PHP is free to install, but you must have administrative rights on the server to do so. The best option for beginners is to select hosting that includes PHP on the server already.

The function *echo* is used to print code to the browser. This will display content on the user's machine after the server processes the page. You can see an example of this here:

```
<!DOCTYPE html>
<html>
    <head>
    <title>My PHP Page</title>
    </head>
    <body>
        <?php
            echo"Hello, PHP!";
        ?>
    </body>
</html>
```

As in the example, each line of PHP ends with a semicolon, just as it does for JavaScript. In fact, all of the concepts used in

JavaScript apply to PHP, with some slight modification. Comments, for example, use // for a single line and /* to */ for multiple lines, just as in JavaScript. The *if* and *switch* statements also use the same syntax in both languages.

The previous example can be formalized to include the *end of line* character (similar to a carriage *return* or *enter* character in text), as follows:

```
<!DOCTYPE html>
<html>
    <head>
    <title>My PHP Page</title>
    </head>
    <body>
        <?php
            echo"Hello, PHP!" . PHP_EOL;
        ?>
    </body>
</html>
```

The variable PHP_EOL is a reserved global variable that represents this *end of line* character. The period operator (.) is used to concatenate strings. Variables in PHP are defined using the dollar sign ($). As in JavaScript, there is no specific data type that must be declared for a variable, so it can store a character, a string, a Boolean value, an integer, or any other valid data type. An example of this is:

```
<!DOCTYPE html>
<html>
    <head>
    <title>My PHP Page</title>
    </head>
    <body>
        <?php
            $mytext = "Hello, PHP!" . PHP_EOL;
            echomytext;
```

```
            ?>
        </body>
</html>
```

7.2.2 Form Processing

ACTIVITY 7.2 – SETTING UP A PHP PAGE

For this activity, you will use the template from the case project to create a PHP page to process the form submission from the contact page. The structure you use should match that of the other pages in the site, but where the content is located, you should add PHP tags and code to produce the statement "Form processing coming soon." Save the page as contact.php. Because of the nature of PHP, you can save this in the same directory as the rest of your HTML pages. If you have a hosting solution already, you should test this page on the server to make sure it works correctly.

Form processing on the server side has slightly different goals from those of form processing on the client side. On the client machine, the goal is to make sure the data is correct and will allow transactions or contact between the client and the Web application to work correctly. On the server, your ultimate goal is to protect the application from malformed or even malicious data. You can still check for errors in content and reject the input at this stage, but the focus should be on making sure the length and content of the input are safe for the application to process.

The first step is to get access to the form data. PHP simplifies this process for you: when you use the POST method of form submission, you can access the name value pairs through the global variable $_POST. This variable is an array that stores the names as index strings and their associated values. For instance, the code to return the *input* value for *myname* from the client is:

$_POST["myname"] You can store this value in another variable or manipulate the value using this reference to the *$_POST* array. You can use this reference to display the form content to the user, to e-mail the content, or to store the content in a database. Before you use it for any of those purposes, though, you should make sure the data is formatted for what is required by the Web application. The data length may not matter for display or e-mail, but it will matter when you are storing information in a database that has size constraints. Even e-mailed data should be screened for unsafe characters. In order to properly scrub the data for use in the Web application, there are three steps that should be performed:

- *Limit the length*: You do not want the size of your data to exceed the size that can be used by the Web application. This does not have to be done for all data, such as the message length for an e-mail body, but it should be considered for each element of the form to determine individually whether this step is needed.

- *Remove unsafe characters*: Unsafe characters are those that can harm the Web application or any of its components. It is a good idea to scrub all of the data for these characters unless they have a specific purpose for being included.

- *Eliminate HTML/XML tags:* This is not always necessary, but the inclusion of tags allows the data to become active within the Web application in which it is processed. For instance, code embedded in <script> and </script> tags can be activated when the code is displayed to the viewer, allowing the client in some cases to take over the Web application or manipulate it. Unless there is a specific case in which the tags should be kept, it is better to eliminate the use of HTML or XML tags in the data.

To process the form data for use, you should start by limiting the length and moving through the steps as needed. As an example, these steps will be performed on the *myname* field of the contact form to demonstrate the process. Assume the *myname* field should be limited to 50 characters based on the typical name size and storage needed for this value to be saved in a database; this should actually be more than enough length for this field, so it is unlikely a name would not fit in this field.

To limit the length of the *myname* field, you would use the *substr* function to create a *substring* of the value that contains only the number of characters you want to include, such as:

```
$_POST["myname"] = substr($_POST["myname"], 0, 50);
```

The parameters in this case specify the string value to use, the starting value, and the number of characters to include beginning with the starting value. Here, *0* is used as the starting value, because the string starts counting with *0* as the first character. The length value of *50* will take 50 characters from the starting value *0*.

 You can test the length of a string in PHP by using the function **strlen**, which takes the string data as its only parameter and returns the number of characters found in the string.

The next step in the process is to remove any unsafe characters from the form data. PHP has a function called *string_replace* that can be used to perform this task. It requires an array of characters to be replaced if there are more than one, so the array must first be defined. This can be done using the list of unsafe characters from the chapter on JavaScript:

```
$unsafe =array(";",""","\"","&","\\");
```

Using this array, the following statement will replace these characters with an empty character (denoted ""), effectively removing the unsafe character from the string:

```
$unsafe = array(";",""","\"","&","\\");
$_POST["myname"] = string_replace($unsafe, "", $_
POST["myname"]);
```

The final step is to remove any HTML or XML tags from the data. PHP has a function that performs this task, called *strip_tags*. It can be used as shown:

```
$_POST["myname"] = strip_tags($_POST["myname"]);
```

Putting all of this together, you can process and display the *myname* field using the following code:

```
<!DOCTYPE html>
```

```html
<html>
    <head>
    <title>Contact Page</title>
    </head>
    <body>
        <?php
            // This will process and display the
myname field
$_POST["myname"] = substr($_POST["myname"], 0, 50);
$unsafe = array(";","'","\"","&","\\");
$_POST["myname"] = string_replace($unsafe, "", ↵
$_POST["myname"]);
$_POST["myname"] = strip_tags($_POST["myname"]); ↵
            echo $_POST["myname"];
        ?>
    </body>
</html>
```

You can test this by setting the *action* attribute of the form tag in *contact.html* to point to the location of the *contact.php* page (such as *action="contact.php"* if the files are both in the same folder). Your site must reside on a server with PHP installed for this to work. You can repeat this process for all of the fields in the form you are trying to process.

ACTIVITY 7.2 – PHP FORM PROCESSING

For this activity, you will use the example code above to process the data from the form contact.html in the case project. You can modify your contact.php page to perform these tasks as needed for every field in the form. The page should display the content that the user submitted. As a challenge, you should display it in a format that will show the meaning of the content. Save your work as part of the case project. If you have a hosting solution already, you should test this page on the server to make sure it works correctly.

7.2.3 E-mailing with PHP

Now that you are able to access and manipulate the data from the form, you can apply it to a useful purpose. For a contact page, it is ideal to e-mail the contact information to an administrator who can then return the contact if needed or log and process the information. The *mail* command in PHP can be used to send e-mail from the server to any valid address.

Not all hosting options allow you to set the e-mail addresses of the sender and receiver. This is a limitation you should investigate with the host prior to selecting your plan. The risk of this functionality is that a Web application may be used for generating unwanted spam, so some hosts either charge a premium rate for this functionality or disable it.

The most complex element of the *mail* function is the header requirement. The easiest way to create this parameter is with a separate variable for storing all of the headers. The header values that must be completed are the *MIME* type, the *content-type* of the e-mail, and the *From* value. Without a *From* value, the *mail* function will return an error. Without a *MIME* type or *content-type* header, the content may not be displayed correctly. The code to build the headers is as follows:

```
$headers = 'MIME-Version: 1.0' . '\r\n';
$headers .= 'Content-type: text/html;
charset=iso-8859-1' . '\r\n';$headers .= 'From: The-
odor Richardson <noreply@wherever.com>' . '\r\n';
```

Note the use of the period (.) as a concatenation operator both within the *assignment* part of the statement and to modify the *assignment* operator to concatenate the left side of the statement to the existing *string* value. The string '\r\n' is a combination of the *return carriage* and *new line* characters; including both will accommodate Windows and Linux servers. If the mail is not being sent or received, you may need to remove the character that is not supported by your server.

The *mail* function takes four parameters: the address of the recipient (*To:*), the *Subject* line, the message body, and the additional headers. An example of this would be:

```
$mailme = mail('to.address@wherever.com', ↵

'This is the subject line', 'This is the message ↵
body.', $headers);
```

The *mail* function returns a *true* or *false* value, so it must be assigned to either a variable or a conditional statement. To put all of this together, the PHP code to process the form field *myname* and e-mail the name to a specified recipient address would be:

```
<!DOCTYPE html>
<html>
    <head>
    <title>Contact Page</title>
    </head>
    <body>
        <?php
            // This will process and display the
myname field
$_POST["myname"] = substr($_POST["myname"], 0, 50);
$unsafe = array(";","'","\"","&","\\");
$_POST["myname"] = string_replace($unsafe, "", ↵
$_POST["myname"]);
$_POST["myname"] = strip_tags($_POST["myname"]);

echo $_POST["myname"];

$headers = 'MIME-Version: 1.0' . '\r\n';
$headers .= 'Content-type: text/html; ↵
charset=iso-8859-1' . '\r\n';
$headers .= 'From: Theodor Richardson <noreply@wher-
```

```
ever.com>' . '\r\n';
$mailme = mail('to.address@wherever.com', ↵
'Contact Entry Information', 'The name field is ' . ↵
$_POST["myname"], $headers);
        ?>
    </body>
</html>
```

Note the concatenation to include the form field value of *myname*. You should expand this example to include all of the form fields in both the form processing and the e-mail body to provide a more complete form-processing solution. The next chapter will explore how to use this data to populate a database.

ACTIVITY 7.3 – E-MAILING WITH PHP

For this activity, you will modify the contact.php file you have been constructing for the case project to process all of the form fields and then e-mail the result to an e-mail address you operate. In the e-mail message, you should include the names of the form fields and the values separated by the new line and carriage return characters. If you have a hosting solution already, you should test this page on the server to make sure it works correctly and verify that you receive the e-mail in the format you specified.

7.3 PERL

Perl has famously been called the "the duct tape of the Internet" by Hassan Schroeder. It is a language that was intended to combine the convenience of shell scripting with the more robust features of full languages like C and C++. It is one of the most commonly used and well-supported server-side languages, as well as one of the oldest in use on the Web. Even when other server-side languages are not supported on a server, Perl is typically available for use. It is not as convenient to use as PHP, and it requires specific invocation of the Perl binary executable file in order to work correctly. Perl is also not as forgiving as PHP, returning only an error message for the page if anything is incorrect in the code. While hosting options allow you to select the server-side languages you want to use, it is beneficial to learn Perl for cases in which you do not have options for hosting, such as preset client servers.

Perl was written by Larry Wall. The name Perl is a retronym, meaning the name itself came first and the expansion of the acronym's letters came later. As with PHP, the real expansion of the Perl retronym is up for debate, since its creator has endorsed both Practical Extraction and Report Language and Pathologically Eclectic Rubbish Lister. Notice as well that Perl is not capitalized like most acronyms.

7.3.1 Perl Basics

Perl can be written in any text editor, just like HTML. The difference with Perl is that it must be formatted in the native coding of the server on which it resides; this is a difference between *return carriage* characters in Windows (typically ANSI encoding) and *new line* characters in Linux (typically UTF-8 encoding). Programs like Notepad++ can change the encoding from one format to another, so you do not have to write the code on the server if you have a conversion program like this. Perl files should be named with the *.pl* extension.

The first line of any Perl text file must be the path to the Perl executable binary file. The common path to Perl is:

```
#!/usr/bin/perl
```

The path given is the most common path to the Perl executable, but this value must match the location of the Perl binary file on the specific server, so there may be instances where this path will not work and you will have to investigate where the binary executable files are stored for the specific server. Hosting solutions will typically provide you with a path if they support Perl.

The function *print* is used to output information to a file stream. If no file stream is specified, the default behavior of *print* is to place the text in the browser. To print the text "Hello, Perl!" in a browser, the following code would be used:

```
#!/usr/bin/perl
print "Hello, Perl!";
```

This is the function you will use to write HTML to the browser from a Perl file. For the case project, you could use the following code in Perl to produce a page similar to the example for PHP:

```
#!/usr/bin/perl

print "<!DOCTYPE html>";
print "<html>";
print "<head>";
print "<title>My Perl Page</title>";
print "</head>";
print "<body>";
print "Hello, Perl!";
print "</body>";
print "</html>";
```

ACTIVITY 7.4 – INVOKING PERL

For this activity, you will create a file using Perl that will produce a Web page on the client machine that matches the template used in your case project. The content section of the page should contain the text "Hello, Perl!" Unlike the case with PHP, you will need to code the HTML that will be produced into the Perl output for the page. You will also have to check the path to the Perl binary to make sure it works. Save the page as hello.pl. If you have a hosting solution already, you should test this page on the server to make sure it works correctly. Comments in Perl are created by using the hash mark (#).

7.3.2 Form Processing

Form processing in Perl is much more complicated than it is in PHP and represents one of the more difficult and involved coding aspects of this text. Before you can use the form data, you must capture the information on the input stream from the browser, named

STDIN. The *read* function can be used to gather information from an input stream and place it in a variable. Variables in Perl are denoted with a dollar sign (*$*) for single variables and the 'at' symbol (@) for arrays. The code to read the posted form information from *STDIN* and place it in the variable called *$buffer* is:

```
read(STDIN, $buffer, $ENV{'CONTENT_LENGTH'});
```

The reserved variable *$ENV{'CONTENT_LENGTH'}* is used to specify the amount of data to read from the input stream based on what is available.

From here, it is necessary to parse the *$buffer* variable for the name and value pairs of the form. The first step is to separate the different pairs from each other using *split*. The *split* function takes the following parameters: a character on which to split a string and the string to split. This function creates an array as its output, which must be further broken down into names and values. The code for processing this deconstruction of the *STDIN* data to name and value pairs is:

```
read(STDIN, $buffer, $ENV{'CONTENT_LENGTH'});

@pairs = split(/&/, $buffer);
foreach $pair (@pairs) {
($name, $value) = split(/=/, $pair);
$FORM{$name} = $value;
}
```

This code must be further complicated to remove the plus signs and Web encoding from the text content of the form data:

```
read(STDIN, $buffer, $ENV{'CONTENT_LENGTH'});

@pairs = split(/&/, $buffer);
foreach $pair (@pairs) {
    ($name, $value) = split(/=/, $pair);
$value =~ tr/+/ /;
    $value =~ s/%([a-fA-F0-9][a-fA-F0-9])/pack("C",
```

```
hex($1))/eg;
    $FORM{$name} = $value;
}
```

This is complex code beyond the scope of beginner programming; for now it is best for you to copy the code and evaluate its meaning as you become more advanced with the language and its use.

The net result of this code is the ability to refer to the form field through the *$FORM* variable. An example of this is shown for referencing the *myname* field in the form from *contact.html:*

```
$FORM{'myname'}
```

The code for making sure the format of the data in the form fields is suitable for use in the Web application is also more complex in Perl. To limit the length of the myname field to 50 characters, you can use the *substr* operator similarly to the way it was used in PHP:

```
$FORM{'myname'} = substr($FORM{'myname'},0,50);
```

To remove unsafe characters, the code uses the substitution operator for regular expressions and an empty substitution string as a replacement. This uses the regular expression list from JavaScript as a basis for removing these unsafe characters:

```
$FORM{'myname'}=~ s/;|'|"|&|\\//g;
```

Finally, to eliminate HTML or XML tags from the form data, you can use another regular expression that identifies tag formatting and replaces it with an empty string. An example of this is:

```
$FORM{'myname'}=~ s/<!--(.|\n)*-->//g;
```

The elimination of unsafe characters and HTML/XML tags can be done inside the main code to produce the *$FORM* variable. Putting all of this together, the most efficient solution (assuming each field will have a different length) is:

```perl
#!/usr/bin/perl

read(STDIN, $buffer, $ENV{'CONTENT_LENGTH'});

@pairs = split(/&/, $buffer);
foreach $pair (@pairs) {
    ($name, $value) = split(/=/, $pair);
$value =~ tr/+/ /;
    $value =~ s/%([a-fA-F0-9][a-fA-F0-9])/pack("C", ↵
hex($1))/eg;
# This eliminates unsafe characters for every field ↵
value
$value = =~ s/;|'|"|&|\\//g;
# This eliminates HTML or XML tags for every field ↵
value
$value =~ s/<!--(.|\n)*-->//g;
    $FORM{$name} = $value;
}

# This must be individualized for each field if ↵
they are different sizes
$FORM{'myname'} = substr($FORM{'myname'},0,50);

print "<!DOCTYPE html>";
print "<html>";
print "<head>";
print "<title>My Perl Page</title>";
print "</head>";
print "<body>";
print$FORM{'myname'};
print "</body>";
print "</html>";
```

E-mailing with Perl

E-mailing information with Perl uses the same *print* function that is used to write output to the browser. Instead of using the default action, though, you will specify an output stream on which to write the content. The wrapper for this structure is:

```
open (MAIL, "|/usr/sbin/sendmail to.address@wher-
ever.com");
print MAIL "This is the email content...";
```

Here the *open* function is used to create a new stream of information; in this case it is opening a path to the e-mail executable on the server. The second part of the string identifying the e-mail path is the address to which the e-mail will be sent. The common path to the e-mail executable *sendmail* is:

```
/usr/sbin/sendmail
```

However, just as with the Perl executable, you must specify the specific path to the *sendmail* executable on the server itself, which may vary from server to server.

Just as you used the *print* function to build the HTML page, you will use it here to build the e-mail headers and message. This should include the *From* and *Subject* lines. After the header, be sure to indicate a double *new line* character (\n \n); this will signify to the e-mail processor that it is has moved from the header to the body of the message. You can see an example of this here:

```
print MAIL "Reply-to: from.address@wherever.com\n";
print MAIL "From: from.address@wherever.com\n";
print MAIL "Subject: This is the subject line\n\n";
print MAIL "This is the message body.";
```

Finally, when the content of the e-mail is complete, you will close the stream, which will send the e-mail message and continue with the execution of the rest of the Perl code. An example of this is:

```
close (MAIL);
```

The complete code for processing and e-mailing the *myname* field of the form from *contact.html* is:

```perl
#!/usr/bin/perl

read(STDIN, $buffer, $ENV{'CONTENT_LENGTH'});

@pairs = split(/&/, $buffer);
foreach $pair (@pairs) {
    ($name, $value) = split(/=/, $pair);
$value =~ tr/+/ /;
    $value =~ s/%([a-fA-F0-9][a-fA-F0-9])/pack("C", ↵
hex($1))/eg;
# This eliminates unsafe characters for every field ↵
value
$value = =~ s/;|'|"|&|\\///g;
# This eliminates HTML or XML tags for every field ↵
value
$value =~ s/<!--(.|\n)*-->//g;
    $FORM{$name} = $value;
}


# This must be individualized for each field if ↵
they are different sizes
$FORM{'myname'} = substr($FORM{'myname'},0,50);

open (MAIL, "|/usr/sbin/sendmail to.address ↵
@wherever.com");
print MAIL "Reply-to: from.address@wherever.com\n";
print MAIL "From: from.address@wherever.com\n";
print MAIL "Subject: Contact Form Information\n\n";
print MAIL "The name of the contact is
$FORM{'myname'}.";
close (MAIL);
```

```
print "<!DOCTYPE html>";
print "<html>";
print "<head>";
print "<title>My Perl Page</title>";
print "</head>";
print "<body>";
print$FORM{ 'myname' };
print "</body>";
print "</html>";
```

Note in the example that including a variable name within a string will replace the name with the variable content at execution, eliminating the need to concatenate strings and variables in Perl.

CHAPTER SUMMARY

This chapter introduced the concept of Web hosting for putting your Web site live on the Internet. Part of the decision for hosting is choosing the server-side languages you want supported for the site. Server-side languages provide you with the ability to preprocess information to deliver personalized, dynamic content to your users as well as to access additional functionality like e-mail messaging. PHP is one of the most popular server-side languages in use; it offers the user the ability to embed the code directly within an HTML page, and it provides powerful tools for accessing databases and generating dynamic content. Perl is another popular language for server-side scripting; though it is not as easy to use as PHP, it is more widely available on both new and old servers. It is worthwhile to learn more than one server-side language. There are other options to choose in this category, such as ASP, which uses Visual Basic as the programming language, and JSP, which uses Java. As you learn more programming in any language, it becomes easier to learn additional languages. The final chapter of this text is devoted to creating and updating databases of information for your Web site. The tool that will be presented for this task is MySQL, which can be used to store data from a Web site easily and works seamlessly with PHP. Combining all of these tools will allow you to create dynamic, engaging, and professional-quality Web sites for yourself and your clients.

CHAPTER KNOWLEDGE CHECK

Which of the following is a valid variable declaration in PHP?

○ **A.** $3 = x;
○ **B.** $x = 3;
○ **C.** x = 3;
○ **D.** All of the above
○ **E.** None of the above

2 Server-side languages process their results when invoked; this means they are not interactive to the client without the client's sending another request to the server.

○ **A.** True
○ **B.** False

3 PHP code can be embedded into any HTML page and will work without changing the file extension of the page.

○ **A.** True
○ **B.** False

4 The exact path to the binary executable file for PHP must be included in every page that uses the language.

○ **A.** True
○ **B.** False

5 PHP code must be written as a standalone file, with no HTML elements included.

○ **A.** True
○ **B.** False

6 Variables in both PHP and Perl are signified by the dollar sign ($) before the actual variable name.

○ **A.** True
○ **B.** False

7 Which of the following functions is used to produce output to the browser in Perl?

○ **A.** open
○ **B.** echo
○ **C.** print
○ **D.** All of the above
○ **E.** None of the above

8 The path to the Perl executable and that to the mail program are the same for all servers.

- ○ **A.** True
- ○ **B.** False

9 The 'at' symbol (@) must be used to denote an array in both PHP and Perl.

- ○ **A.** True
- ○ **B.** False

10 Which of the following represents the new line character in both PHP and Perl?

- ○ **A.** \r
- ○ **B.** \n
- ○ **C.** \g
- ○ **D.** \s
- ○ **E.** None of the above

CHAPTER PROJECTS

Project 1: Personal Web Site

For this project, you should create a form processing solution for the contact page of your site. It should test the input sent by the user and make sure it will not harm the server. This test should be performed on the client side and again on the server side. The results should be sent to your e-mail address after the form is processed. Find hosting for your site and test the code to process the contact form.

Project 2: Resort Web Site

For this project, you should create a form processing solution for the contact page of your site. It should test the input sent by the user and make sure it will not harm the server. This test should be performed on the client side and again on the server side. The results should be sent to your email address after the form is processed. Find hosting for your site and test the code to process the contact form.

CHAPTER EXERCISES

1. Since the server-side languages execute linearly, is there a need to define functions in these languages, or should everything be written to execute once as the code is interpreted or compiled? Use examples to justify your answer.

2. Explain the purpose of creating external files for inclusion in server-side languages. What benefit does it provide to have these additional files, and when would they be useful? Use examples to justify your answer.

3. Write a loop in either PHP or Perl to produce the numbers *1* through *10*. How does this compare to the syntax used for producing this output in JavaScript?

4. Briefly explain the purpose of the *end of line* character. Give two examples of when it should be used.

5. Write an *if-else* statement in PHP or Perl to determine if the number stored in a variable is greater than *5* and state the results as output. How does the syntax of this statement compare to that needed to produce the same result in JavaScript?

6. Write a *switch* statement in PHP or Perl to output the day of the week based on a numeric value stored in a variable. How does the syntax of this statement compare to that needed to produce the same result in JavaScript?

7. Compare the variable declaration process in PHP and Perl. How does the syntax of the two compare? How does a variable type get determined in both languages? Use examples to support your answer.

8. Compare and contrast the syntax used in PHP and Perl for either form processing or sending e-mail. Which language offers the most convenience? Which language is more compact? Explain the differences and justify your answer.

9. Identify the necessary information needed to create a functional Perl file for use on a Web server. What steps must be taken with the file to allow it to run correctly on the server? Briefly explain your answer.

10. Compare the syntax of PHP to that of either ASP or JSP for embedding code in an HTML document. What is the benefit of being able to embed dynamic content in a page? Explain your answer using examples.

CHAPTER REVIEW QUESTIONS

1. Research at least three options for hosting a Web site. Compare the three options in terms of cost, bandwidth, space, and languages supported. Which option is the best in terms of this comparison and why? Are these criteria sufficient to evaluate a Web hosting solution? Why or why not?

2. Choose a server-side language other than PHP or Perl and compare its basic use and convenience to those of PHP. What are the similarities of the language you chose and PHP? What are the differences? Choose which language you think would be better for use on a Web site and justify your answer.

3. Since the source code of a server-side language is typically hidden from the client, what is the purpose of adding comments to the source code for these languages? Justify

your answer and give two examples of when this would be useful or necessary.

4. Products like Visual Studio.NET allow different modules of code written in different languages to communicate with each other. What is the purpose of using multiple programming languages for a Web application? When would this be useful? Justify your answer with examples.

5. Explain in your own words why it is important to perform form validation on both the client side and the server side in a Web application. What are the potential consequences if either side is not tested for valid formatting and unsafe characters? Give examples to support your answer.

6. Briefly explain the difference between JavaScript's *innerHTML* method and the output methods of either PHP or Perl. When are these invoked to change the content of the page, and what triggers the use of each method? Give examples to support your answer.

7. Briefly explain the reason that languages like PHP and Perl can be used to send e-mail from a server to a computer but JavaScript is not capable of generating and sending e-mail on the client side. What effect would it have if JavaScript had that capability?

8. Compare the methods of access to form data in JavaScript and either PHP or Perl. How is the form data accessed? What is the origin of the form data in both cases? Use examples to support your answer.

9. Perl has a steeper learning curve than PHP, but it is still widely used. Use the Internet to research the use of Perl and determine reasons for its continued popularity even with simpler options like PHP available. Justify your position.

10. When is it a good practice to e-mail a copy of the information a user submits in a form back to the user who submitted it? Give at least two examples of when this would be a good practice and two examples of when this would not be a good practice. Justify your answer.

CHAPTER
8

MySQL

Data management is an essential task for most interactive Web sites, especially those with an e-commerce element. One of the most powerful tools for updating and retrieving data from a relational database is Structured Query Language (SQL). One of the most popular choices for integrating databases with the power of SQL into a Web site is MySQL, which can be installed on almost any server. Languages like PHP have inherent functions to let you connect to MySQL easily, which will be the focus of this chapter. Once you have completed this chapter, you should be able to:

- Understand the basic syntax of SQL

- Understand the basic functionality of MySQL

- Use PHP to store and retrieve information from a MySQL database

8.1 MYSQL

MySQL (*www.mysql.com*) is currently the most popular open source database software used in Web sites. Adding MySQL to a server or choosing a hosting service with MySQL installed will allow you to create and manage databases from the server-side languages you learned about in the previous chapter. PHP in particular has a very simple interface for accessing a MySQL database. The construction of databases is a complex process that is beyond the scope of this book, so this chapter will focus on a specific example for the case project that can be adapted for more complex situations as you learn more in the field of database design and practice with the other Web languages for creating more complex Web applications.

MySQL is one of the component software pieces associated with the common LAMP server configuration, which stands for Linux, Apache™, MySQL, and PHP/Perl. The configuration of the Apache server is a separate topic, but you should have the tools and skills to develop Web sites for a LAMP server when you have completed all of the objectives in this text.

8.1.1 MySQL Data Types

A database is composed of *tables*. Each table represents a closely coupled grouping of similar information, such as a name, an address, and a phone number grouped as contact information. Each of the pieces of data in the table is called a *field*. In the prior example, the *phone number* element would be a field. When creating a table in MySQL, you need to consider which fields you will need to store the data. In the example for this chapter, you will construct the table to store the contact information from the contact page of the case project. The actual storage will take place in the server-side page you wrote to process the form data.

A **database** is a collection of interrelated data organized into tables of grouped information. The most common type of database in use is the **relational database**, which specifies data connections as relationships between fields in different tables of the database. MySQL is a **relational database management system**, or RDMS.

A **table** is a group of related data elements, or fields, which forms a cohesive and specific data set with some meaning in an application. The columns represent fields in the data, and the rows represent specific entries in the table.

A **field** is a single piece of data that is included in a table. The field represents the column heading, and the specific entries are rows under this heading. Fields require a data type to determine how to treat the values stored in them.

A database **entry** is a row of data in a table. The values in each column of an entry specify a single instance of the defined field.

Just like variables, each field in a MySQL table needs to have a data type defined. This specifies what kind of information will be stored in the field and how the database should treat the raw data. The common data types for MySQL which you are likely to encounter are:

- *Boolean value:* This represents either *true* or *false,* or, in binary, *1* or *0*, respectively. The specification for a Boolean value in MySQL is either *BOOL* or *BOOLEAN*.

- *Integer:* An integer is any whole number (counting number), with no decimal component. The integer specification in MySQL requires a display width, which in this case is the number of digits in the value. The specification for an integer in MySQL is *INT(n)*, where *n* is the number of digits allowed. There are variations of the integer data type that are supported (such as *TINYINT*), which may be needed when space or efficiency are a concern in the application.

- *Decimal:* The decimal data type is used for values that contain a decimal component. The specification for a decimal value in MySQL is either *DECIMAL(n)* or *DEC(n),* where *n* again represents the allowed number of digits in the value. The variation *DEC(n, d)* allows you to specify *d* as the number of digits allowed in the decimal component of the value. Like integers, decimal values have variations (such as *FLOAT*) for specifying other value ranges.

- *Characters and strings*: Characters and strings in MySQL are both stored in the same data type, in which the number of characters allowed is specified as n. The data type *CHAR(n)* will allow only fixed-length strings with n characters; if the stored value is smaller than the fixed value, it will be right-padded with spaces. The more versatile *VARCHAR(n)* allows strings of variable length up to length n; this is the most common storage mechanism for text fields, such as the contact entries you will record in the sample database. For longer text, you can specify a *TEXT(n)* field, which has a higher storage capacity: up to 65,535 characters, compared to the *VARCHAR* maximum of 255. Using *TEXT* as a data type can be wasteful, though, if it is not needed. Other variations of text, such as *BLOB,* also exist in MySQL for more specialized purposes.

Other data types exist in MySQL; the list here represents only the most commonly used types you are likely to encounter as you begin your work as a Web developer. For instance, there are data types for *DATE* and *TIME* to record these specific data values, which can be recorded as either strings or numbers. This list is enough to get you started with using MySQL, but it is nowhere near a complete listing of all of the available options. Whenever you create a database, you need to consider the data storage carefully.

8.1.2 Creating a MySQL Database

Most hosting solutions will offer you a graphical user Interface (GUI) for creating and modifying MySQL tables. The example shown in this chapter is from *GoDaddy.com,* which provides a GUI from Starfield® Technologies, Inc. Other solutions may be text-based, which would give you an input/output stream that would allow you to configure MySQL directly. For this reason, both the graphic form of the table and the SQL code will be presented, so you can perform this task in either environment. Regardless of the means of creating the table, the most important consideration is the names and types of the fields you will include in your table.

The database should govern part of your form processing. Specifically, the length checks on the field values should conform to the length allowed by the database. Allowing fields with a length greater than the length of the field in the database is inviting errors and retrieval problems when you attempt to store and use the data from the user. This has to be enforced on the front end (with JavaScript error detection) and strictly enforced on the server side (with PHP or Perl); values with a higher length than the allowed storage limit must be either rejected with no storage or truncated to fit within the size allowed by the database.

For the *contact.html* form in the case project, the following fields should be stored in the database:

- *E-mail*: This is the e-mail entry on the form; it will always be text. A rough size of 50 would be a starting point for allocating this field. It should be given the data type VARCHAR(50).

- *Salutation*: This is the greeting given along with the name. The maximum length of the preset options for this field is currently 4, but this may not be an exhaustive list for international users. Therefore, this will be allocated as VARCHAR(5) to allow for any unknown additions needed later. This is fine here, since the database size will remain small, but it may be a consideration when the records will number into the hundreds or thousands.

- *Name*: Since this field contains a first and a last name (which is typically not recommended, since they are distinct data elements), the length of 50 should account for most names. This will be allocated as VARCHAR(50); the testing is already in place to be certain of this limit in the PHP and Perl examples from the previous chapter.

- *Method*: There are only two options for this field, and both contain 5 letters. Therefore, this field should be allocated as VARCHAR(5).

- *Phone*: The variation in formatting of phone numbers in different countries means there should be extra space allocated for international numbers and hyphens. A rough size of 15 characters should suffice for most of these variations. This size can be adjusted later, but it can only contract and not expand from the values already stored in the table.

- *Subscribe*: This is a simple yes-or-no item based on whether the box is checked or not. Therefore, it is a good candidate for BOOL, where TRUE means the subscribe box was checked and FALSE means it was not.

- *Message*: This represents the full text of the message the customer wants to send. It will therefore be the longest field in the contact entry. It is a good candidate for the TEXT data type, though it is wise to limit its size in the form processing stage in both JavaScript and the server-side language.

Figure 8.1 shows the result of creating this table. Note that the SQL statement that created the table is shown above the structure information for the table itself.

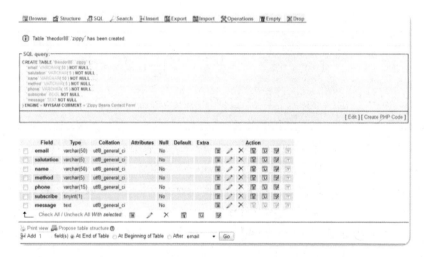

▲ **FIGURE 8.1** Sample Table for the Zippy Beans Contact Form

One final element that is required for any MySQL table is a *primary key*. This is a means of organizing the information in a table and referring to a specific record. The selection of a primary key is typically a complicated process. In this instance, there are no good candidates from the existing data for creating a primary key. Therefore, another field is needed for this table, to complement the record and create a primary key. The combination of the submission date/time and the e-mail information makes a unique identifier for this information.

The submission date should be added to the table as the field *submission* and stored as *VARCHAR(25)*. Most date formats are not 25 characters in length, but this will account for any time inclusion on the date/time stamp from the language used to create and store the date. This field can be added via the GUI interface or via SQL. The full SQL statement for creating this table is:

```
CREATE TABLE `your_schema_name_here`, `zippy` (
    `submission` VARCHAR(25) NOT NULL,
    `email` VARCHAR(50) NOT NULL,
    `salutation` VARCHAR(5) NOT NULL,
    `name` VARCHAR(50) NOT NULL,
    `method` VARCHAR(5) NOT NULL,
    `phone` VARCHAR(15) NOT NULL,
    `subscribe` BOOL NOT NULL,
    `message` TEXT NOT NULL,
) ENGINE = MYSIAM COMMENT = 'Zippy Beans Contact Form'
```

Note that you will need to specify your own schema information (which is typically your account name on the server) in the placeholder that says *your_schema_name_here*.

There are **DATETIME**, **DATE**, and **TIME** data types available in MySQL for storing date and time information, but converting between these data types and the server-side languages can be a complex process. For that reason, a simple **VARCHAR** data type is used for the **submission** field.

The primary key can be added visually using the GUI or via SQL with the following statement:

```
ALTER TABLE `zippy` ADD PRIMARY KEY ( `submission` ,
`email` )
```

Now that these steps are completed, the table is ready for use. In order to use this table for data storage and retrieval, you will need to understand the syntax of SQL queries and the means of calling the database in the server-side language.

8.2 STRUCTURED QUERY LANGUAGE (SQL)

Structured Query Language (SQL) is the most widely used database language today. SQL has an intuitive syntax and tremendous power. It has the ability to create tables, delete tables, add records, modify records, and delete records within an RDMS. Despite the power of this language, you will find it used in Web design for three main purposes: selecting (retrieving) data, updating data, and adding data within existing tables. There may be exceptions to this, but these activities will allow you to get a basic understanding of the SQL structure and perform most of the tasks you need in most Web applications.

8.2.1 Select Queries

The first query you should learn in SQL is a *select* query; this will be used to retrieve data from the database and return it to your Web application for use (such as display). A basic *select* query has two keywords: *SELECT* and *FROM*. The syntax of this query is:

```
SELECT x FROM y
```

Here, x is the field (or fields) you want to retrieve and y is the name of the table from which you want to retrieve them. This type of query will return all of the results in the table. To limit the items returned to a specific record, you need to add the *WHERE* clause, as follows:

```
SELECT x FROM y WHERE z
```

In this case, *z* is the condition that is applied to a record and the record is returned only if the condition is true. An example of this type of query to return the *name* field from the database table you created earlier for an e-mail address of *anyone@somewhere.com* would be:

```
SELECT name FROM zippy WHERE email = 'anyone@some-
where.com'
```

You should note that this may not produce a unique record, because the e-mail address is not the entire primary key for the record. You may have to specify additional conditions for this to return a unique value.

Multiple fields can be selected in a single **select** query by separating the field names with commas. Similarly, multiple clauses can be added to a **WHERE** clause; each condition must be joined with either **AND** or **OR**. Parentheses must be used to create complex conditions.

8.2.2 Update Queries

Update queries are used to modify data that exists within a table. The *update* query uses three keywords: *UPDATE, SET,* and *WHERE.* You should be familiar with the *WHERE* clause already. *UPDATE* specifies the table, and *SET* specifies the field (or fields) to be altered. The basic syntax of an update query is:

```
UPDATE y SET x WHERE z
```

From this example, *y* still represents the table value, *x* represents the field and the value to which it is being set, and *z* represents the condition. If *z* specifies multiple records, each of them will be updated. An example of this to update the name for all entries where the e-mail address is *anyone@somewhere.com* would be:

```
UPDATE zippy SET name = 'Bob' WHERE email = 'anyone@
somewhere.com'
```

8.2.3 Insert Queries

The insert query is used to add a new record in an existing table. This will be the type of query you will use to store new records from the contact form in the database. The structure of an *insert* query in SQL is:

```
INSERT INTO y (x) VALUES (v)
```

In this example, *y* is the table name, *x* is the field (or list of fields separated by commas), and *v* is the value (or list of respective values separated by commas). In this format, the number of entries in *x* and in *v* must be identical for the query to be processed without an error. An example of this for storing a new name in the database would be:

```
INSERT INTO zippy (submission, email, name) VALUES ⏎
('12/12/12','anyone@somewhere.com','Bob')
```

The values listed will be stored in the same order as the names of the specified fields.

The primary key must be included for an **INSERT** statement in SQL to work. In the sample case, every record added must include an e-mail address and a date of submission.

8.3 USING MYSQL WITH PHP

PHP has a convenient toolset for utilizing MySQL databases. This requires the database to be connected to the PHP page; once this is done, data can pass freely between PHP and MySQL in the form of SQL statements sent to MySQL and data lines returned from MySQL. The data returned from a MySQL database must be parsed for use in the PHP program, and the SQL statements have specific functions which pass them to MySQL. In this section, you will learn how to connect to a MySQL database, store data in a table, and retrieve and use data from a table with PHP.

8.3.1 Accessing a MySQL Database

PHP has a single function for connecting to a MySQL database: *mysql_connect.* In order for this to work, you need to supply three pieces of information:

- *URL of the database:* This is the Web address of the MySQL program. This should be provided for you if you choose a hosting option.

- *User name:* This is the user name for your account in MySQL. This has to be coded into the PHP page in order for the connection to be made. You generally choose your user name when configuring the MySQL database.

- *Password:* This is the password for your account in MySQL. This also has to be coded into the PHP page, so you should choose a password that is used only for this account and nowhere else, in case the PHP source code is compromised. If you change your password in MySQL, you will have to change it in the PHP page as well for it to continue working.

All three of these values should be input into the *mysql_connect* function as strings. The function does return a value indicating either a link value if the connection succeeds or *FALSE* if the connection fails. The format of this command is:

```
$link = mysql_connect("hostaddress","username",
"password");
```

Here, *hostaddress* is the URL of MySQL on the server, *username* is the actual user name you use to connect to MySQL, and *password* is the password for your MySQL account. It may be better to create variables for each of these values, so they can be changed more easily later. An example of the command for connecting to the MySQL database within a PHP page with this approach is:

```
$hostaddress = "hostaddress";
$username = "username";
$password = "password";
$link = mysql_connect($hostaddress, $username,
$password);
```

You can add simple validation code to determine if the link was a success or a failure based on the returned value. One possible solution for this is:

```
$hostaddress = "hostaddress";
$username = "username";
$password = "password";
$link = mysql_connect($hostaddress, $username,
$password);
if (!$link) {
    // This is the fail case for the connection...
}
```

Here, the value of *$link* is inverted, so the conditional statement will execute to account for the error only if *$link* is false.

The remaining step is to select the database within the account after the connection is established. Most of the time, you will create a new database for each project unless a limit on databases or tables is imposed by the hosting provider. If you are using shared database hosting, this may be just the account name. If you have multiple databases, then you should select the one that is used for the relevant project. Note that this is the name of the overall database and not a single table within the database. The command in PHP to select a MySQL database is:

```
mysql_select_db("database_name");
```

Here, *database_name* is just the actual name of the database you are selecting for the PHP page to use. If you invoke this function when the MySQL connection attempt has failed, it will generate an error.

Once the connection has been established and the database has been selected, you can run queries against the database as often as needed during the execution of the page. Every new invocation of the page (or any other page on the site) will require a new connection to the database. When you are finished with the connection, you should close it with the function:

```
mysql_close($link);
```

The *$link* value referenced is the returned variable from establishing the original connection to MySQL.

8.3.2 Storing Data in a MySQL Database

With the connection to the MySQL database established, you are able to run queries against the database as described in Section 8.2 of this chapter. The query inputs in the PHP commands to access MySQL all take string data as input, meaning that you can construct the SQL queries in a *string* variable and then reference the variable if it is easier to follow.

The *insert* query will be used to store the data from the form in the database. The *submission* entry will require a date/time stamp to be generated when the form is submitted. An example of PHP code to create this *date* format is:

```
$submission_date = date("m/d/y H:i:s");
```

The formatting string can be modified to provide different interpretations of the date/time. By default, the *date* function operates on the current Unix® timestamp. The form data itself should still be referenced the same way it was in the previous chapter.

The function to run a SQL query to store data is *mysql_query*; this function will again return a value (which is sensitive to the context of the query) and will return *FALSE* if the query does not succeed. The code to store the values in the MySQL database from the *contact.html* form is:

```
$submission_date = date("m/d/y H:i:s");
```

```
$query = "INSERT INTO zippy (submission, email, sal-
utation, name, method, phone, message) VALUES ('" .
$submission_date . "','" . ↵$_POST['email']) ."','"
. $_POST['salutation'] . "','" . ↵
$_POST['name'] . "','" . $_POST['preference'] .
"','" . ↵
$_POST['phone'] . "','" . $_POST['message'] . "')";


$result = mysql_query($query);
```

The values entered are all strings, so they need to be surrounded
with single quotation marks, since the overall query string is surrounded with double quotation marks. Note the use of concatenation
on the overall string to get the variable data from PHP. It is advis-
able to use a conditional evaluation to test whether the query was
successful.

ACTIVITY 8.3 – STORING CONTACT INFORMATION

For this activity, you will modify the PHP page you created to
process the contact.html form input from users. You should
use the code examples given to build an appropriate query to
store the information in your live database and test this connection by submitting form data through the contact.html page
and viewing the output. Be sure to include the verification testing for the query with a visual output showing that the query
attempt has failed.

8.3.3 Retrieving Data from a MySQL Database

The *select* query will be used to retrieve stored data from the
MySQL database for use in your PHP Web application. In the sample
case, the information is stored using the e-mail address and submission date of the contact as an index to identify unique records. Since
the submission date is being generated within the same PHP page,
this will be a simple way to recall the data. However, in real cases, it

may be necessary to identify other criteria for this data to return a unique record or you may need to move through several records to identify the correct result you want to use.

As it is in the storage process, the *mysql_query* is used to run the SQL query. This time, the data returned will be the actual records that match the criteria. For this usage, you may want only a subset of the data stored, such as the name and message. You can specify only these fields in the *select* query and use the submission date and the e-mail as the criteria to identify the record. One example of a *select* query to return this information for the case project example is:

```
$submission_date = date("m/d/y H:i:s");
$query = "SELECT name, message FROM zippy WHERE sub-
mission = '" . ⏎$submission_date . "' AND email = '"
. $_POST['email']) ."'";


$result = mysql_query($query);
```

The variable *$result* now contains all of the returned records or the *FALSE* result if the query failed. It is always advisable to test for the *FALSE* case when you run a SQL query.

In order to process the results, you must first extract each record from the returned set. This is accomplished using the *mysql_fetch_array* function, which returns an array of strings matching the order of the parameters given in the *select* query. Every time this function is called, it will pull out the first available record and remove it from the set. An example of this is:

```
$submission_date = date("m/d/y H:i:s");
$query = "SELECT name, message FROM zippy WHERE sub-
mission = '" . ⏎$submission_date . "' AND email = '"
. $_POST['email']) ."'";


$result = mysql_query($query);
$row = mysql_fetch_array($result);
```

If this code executes and successfully returns a record, *$row* is now an array in which *$row[0]* contains the name and *$row[1]* contains the message.

If there are no records returned, it is imperative that this be determined before use of any of the *array* values. Using an *array* value if the record is empty will cause an error in the PHP application. The conditional evaluation *isset* can be used to determine whether the variable contains data (in this circumstance and others). One test for the successful extraction of a record in such a case is:

```
$submission_date = date("m/d/y H:i:s");
$query = "SELECT name, message FROM zippy WHERE sub-
mission = '" . ↵$submission_date . "' AND email = '"
. $_POST['email'] ."'";

$result = mysql_query($query);
$row = mysql_fetch_array($result);
if (isset($row)) {
    // The record is present and can be used...
} else {
    // The record is not present and the row is empty...
}
```

You should plan a fail case for the application if the SQL queries do not work, since any part of the application that depends on the result will not work properly.

ACTIVITY 8.4 – RETRIEVING CONTACT INFORMATION

For this activity, you will modify the PHP page you created to process the contact.html form input from users. You should use the code examples given to retrieve the data that was just stored in the database to verify that it was stored correctly. You should display the data to the user from the database rather than the form itself to show that the storage process was successful. Be sure to include the verification testing for the query with a visual output showing that the query attempt has failed or that the record was not returned.

CHAPTER SUMMARY

This chapter introduced MySQL as a possible RDMS for a Web application. This is currently the most popular open source database solution used on the Web. The language used to power interactions with MySQL is Structured Query Language (SQL). SQL is a powerful database language used in Web applications and standalone databases in businesses worldwide. The basic actions of SQL are creating and deleting tables and storing, updating, and retrieving records within tables in a given database. PHP provides a powerful toolset for interacting with MySQL using the SQL language. This chapter covered the basic operations of using PHP and MySQL to create a Web application, but there is much more to learn in both of these areas. This text has covered the main tools needed to create a dynamic and modern Web site through both the front-end design and the back-end programming. Many of these languages have numerous expansions and nuances that come with experience, research, and use. You should now be on your way to designing and developing professional Web pages and complete Web applications!

CHAPTER KNOWLEDGE CHECK

Which of the following is not a text data type in MySQL?

- ○ **A.** TEXT
- ○ **B.** CHAR
- ○ **C.** VARCHAR
- ○ **D.** BLOB
- ○ **E.** All of the above
- ○ **F.** None of the above

2

Which of the following is not a reserved word in SQL?

- ○ **A.** SELECT
- ○ **B.** FROM
- ○ **C.** WHERE
- ○ **D.** INSERT
- ○ **E.** All of the above
- ○ **F.** None of the above

3

Multiple fields can be selected in a single SQL query by separating the values with a ____.

- ○ **A.** comma
- ○ **B.** period
- ○ **C.** semicolon
- ○ **D.** slash

4

The numerical value in a MySQL data type declaration specifies the number of characters or digits that can be stored in the field.

- ○ **A.** True
- ○ **B.** False

5

Data values specified in a SQL *insert* query are all specified as strings, regardless of how they are stored in the database.

- ○ **A.** True
- ○ **B.** False

6

The ____ clause specifies the conditions for identifying a record in SQL.

- ○ **A.** SELECT
- ○ **B.** WHERE
- ○ **C.** FROM
- ○ **D.** WHILE
- ○ **E.** None of the above

7 The username and password for the MySQL account must be coded into the PHP program in order for it to access the database.

- ○ **A.** True
- ○ **B.** False

8 Which of the following is not a valid PHP function for working with MySQL?

- ○ **A.** mysql_query
- ○ **B.** mysql_close
- ○ **C.** mysql_connect
- ○ **D.** All of the above
- ○ **E.** None of the above

9 The conditional *isset* is used in PHP to determine whether a variable has been assigned data by returning *TRUE* or *FALSE*.

- ○ **A.** True
- ○ **B.** False

10 A SQL query can return multiple records at the same time.

- ○ **A.** True
- ○ **B.** False

CHAPTER PROJECTS

Project 1: Personal Web Site

For this project, you should create a database table to store the contact information from the contact form and process that form using PHP. The data results should be e-mailed to your e-mail address and stored in the database for later use. Document your code to indicate the actions taken in PHP. Test and verify your solution.

Project 2: Resort Web Site

For this project, you should create a database table to store the contact information from the contact form and process that form using PHP. The data results should be e-mailed to your e-mail address and stored in the database for later use. Document your code to indicate the actions taken in PHP. Test and verify your solution.

CHAPTER EXERCISES

1. What is the benefit of creating the database access code as a separate PHP page? Research the inclusion of PHP pages in other pages and convert the database access code to its own page. If this included page is used to initiate a connection to the database, where should the database be closed in the code?

2. The subscription choice was omitted from the storage code in the example in this chapter. Compose JavaScript or PHP code to determine if the checkbox is checked so the value passed to the database will be TRUE/FALSE or 1/0. Add this element into the insert query used to store the contact form data in the database.

3. Explain the benefit of storing and then retrieving the same data to and from a database within the same page. Is this always necessary for testing? Why or why not?

4. Describe the difference in efficiency and convenience between creating the query string directly inside the PHP function and creating it as an external variable. List benefits and drawbacks of each approach.

5. Write a query and loop to return and parse all records from the database and display them as a contact record. What information should be included publicly on this page, and what should be kept hidden? Explain your answer.

6. Write a PHP statement to update the names in the database to a single value regardless of the name given. When would this type of update script be useful? Would a modified form of this update be more usable for practical purposes?

7. Write a PHP statement to delete a record that meets certain criteria (such as a matching e-mail address) from the database. What is the danger of using this type of query? When would this be useful in a Web application? Justify your answer.

8. Write a select query with a complex WHERE clause involving both AND and OR. Test this statement in PHP to verify that it works. What is the benefit of using OR for returning records? Can OR clauses ever uniquely identify just one record? Explain your answer.

9. List at least three factors that should be used to determine what data type is used for a field in a MySQL database. Are these factors common to all database and programming language data type considerations? Why or why not?

10. Use the Internet to research the use of mysql_query in PHP. What are the possible return values for this function? Is there a limitation on the types of queries that can be used, or does it accommodate all of the different SQL query types? Explain your answer.

CHAPTER REVIEW QUESTIONS

1. Define a relational database in your own words. What are the benefits of this type of database? Is this type of database able to handle most application data adequately? Why or why not?

2. Briefly explain the main components of a LAMP stack as a server configuration. What is the purpose of each component, and how do they represent a complete Web application environment when combined?

3. Explain in your own words the benefit of having a common language like SQL for use across multiple commercial database systems. What would happen if each database system had its own query language? How would this affect development of Web applications?

4. Research the use of MySQL with Perl. What tools does Perl provide for connecting to the database and running queries on the database once it is connected? Provide a brief comparison between MySQL use in PHP and Perl.

5. What would be the consequence of using SQL queries to create database tables within Web applications? Explain in your own words why this is not considered a good practice in Web design?

6. Why is it important to test whether each query has successfully completed in a Web application? What can happen to a Web application if data is expected from a query and only the *FALSE* value is returned? Give examples to support your answer.

7. Give at least two additional uses for *isset* in a Web application aside from testing whether a record is present in a MySQL result. Would this be an essential inclusion in each example, or does it just represent a best practice? Explain your answer.

8. Research SQL queries and briefly describe two additional query types that were not included in this chapter. When and how is each of these queries used?

9. Why is it necessary for a MySQL database to have a URL even when it resides on the same server as the PHP page that is accessing it? Justify your answer with examples.

10. Why is it important for a PHP page to have the account user name and password to access a database? Is there an alternative approach that would still restrict access to just authorized pages without requiring this information? How can this issue be managed administratively to minimize the impact of having to code this information within the application?

APPENDIX

A

Selected Answers

Chapter 1

Chapter Knowledge Check

1. d
3. c
5. c
7. b
9. b

Chapter Review Questions

3. The intended audience in the case of a rock band would be fans of the band who wish to learn more, purchase tickets, or find out the latest news on the band. A good place to start would be to research the market to which the band appeals. Questions like "Where do they play most often?" and "What bands play with them?" will help define the audience in this case.

5. There are wide arrays of sites that use too many colors in the palette. There should be a limit of two primary colors and an accent color to be the most appealing. Too many colors make the site look sloppy and unprofessional. A site that has this should condense its color scheme with the most relevant colors.

7. This is a very individual assignment. An ideal palette in this case is two adjacent colors in the color wheel and a complementary color, but the opinions on this differ in graphic design.

As long as there is a defense for it and the colors have the potential of creating a high level of contrast while still appearing to fit together (such as two cool colors and a warm color or two warm colors and a cool color), then the palette can work. Colors that all contrast should be avoided.

Chapter 2

Chapter Knowledge Check

1. c
3. b
5. a
7. b
9. b

Chapter Review Questions

3. One strategy for bringing a functional prototype to completion would be to iteratively add more functionality until the entire site is implemented. The prototype should only be shown to the client when there is a milestone of accomplishment, such as a working application within the site; the client does not need to see every iteration or small change to the site. Some of the factors affecting the schedule would be the level of coding needed to implement the site, server issues, and language issues. Showing a prototype too often will lessen the impact of the development and may cause the client to become irritated with the pestering for approval. Not showing the client often enough may cause the project to deviate from what the client expected, causing significant re-development needs and delays to the project.

5. The client has likely worked very hard at establishing their image as a company. They will likely want any site that is developed to build from that impression rather than deviate into something new. Consider companies that are popular and

well-known; what color schemes and logos do they use and what would you expect on one of their sites? The same principle applies with other clients as well.

7. Color coding in the HTML allows you to quickly identify what tags are being used and it separates the code from the text. The structure of the page should be clearer if you can look at the nesting of tags with the contents abstracted.

Chapter 3

Chapter Knowledge Check

1. e
3. b
5. c
7. a
9. b

Chapter Review Questions

3. Placeholder content in a <div> layout allows you to see visually where the <div> is placed on the page before you have the content to complete it. A <div> could be empty if it contains dynamic content that is only filled under certain conditions. It will typically contain some information or a graphic, though.

5. The images in the final design should be clear and sized to fit the location where they appear. Any lower or higher size or resolution will either cause the image to display poorly or it will be a waste of bandwidth. The visual prototype images are often low quality and constructed quickly to be discarded. The final images need to be high quality.

7. An <img> tag can link to a longer description of images. This can be useful for browsers for the visually impaired, which read descriptions of the image. It can also be helpful for those looking for more information about the image.

Chapter 4

1. d
3. c
5. e
7. c
9. c

Chapter Review Questions

3. It is important for older browsers to "fail gracefully" and ignore a style command that they do not recognize because it allows the newer browsers to use the evolving standards without worrying about how older browsers will treat it. The newer browsers will display the content better and the older browsers will process it as well as they can. If the older browsers did not fail gracefully, the standards would be limited by the older browsers still in use because it would preclude the population using it from viewing newer pages that did not fit their old standard.

5. Using an external style sheet for a site allows every page to keep the same formatting and display. It allows pages to be uniform and connects them visually and stylistically. The only drawback would be to use it extensively for page-specific styles. This may cause confusion if there are too many specific styles defined in the use. These work best when they contain the common elements for multiple pages and allow the individual pages to use the unique styles that only apply to that page.

7. Either positioning or display could be argued as the most important benefit of CSS. Both of these aspects are incredibly powerful and are beyond the scope of simple HTML code (requiring the use of deprecated tags and attributes to accomplish).

Chapter 5

Chapter Knowledge Check

1. d
3. b
5. e
7. a
9. d

Chapter Review Questions

3. Using hyperlinks to reference IDs of tags within the same page allows you to establish bookmarks within a page to jump to specific content. In a long document such a history or technical specification, you could allow users to jump to a specific section or timeframe. Numerous other applications exist for this.

5. It is important to limit the use of plug-in content on a Web page because not every user will have the plug-in installed. The risk you run when adding plug-in content that is not inherently supported by the Web browser itself is that the content will not be seen and the user may not know how to access it. One example of this is the use of Adobe Flash content on a mobile device which cannot support the plug-in. This limits the audience for the content.

7. A *favicon* in a Web site is an icon that displays next to the name of the page in a browser. It helps to define site branding and establish consistency across pages. It is a good idea to have a *favicon* for a business but it can be a small item that shows experience and knowledge even on a personal site.

Chapter 6

Chapter Knowledge Check

1. d
3. a

5.　d

7.　a

9.　c

3.　Coding libraries like jQuery provide reusable code that is known to work in various environments. This type of library can save a lot of time in re-developing existing functions and functionality.

5.　A programming language has to be compiled into machine code before execution but a scripting language is interpreted dynamically as it is called. JavaScript is considered a scripting language because it is executed on the client machine within the browser without being compiled.

7.　All of the different loop types in JavaScript are relatively interchangeable. The parameters of each can be adjusted to perform the same behavior, but there are more efficient loops for specific tasks than others.

Chapter 7

Chapter Knowledge Check

1.　b

3.　b

5.　b

7.　c

9.　b

Chapter Review Questions

3.　Since the source code of a server-side language is typically hidden from the client, the purpose of adding comments to the source code for these languages is for later maintenance and support. Proper documentation can also allow for reuse of the code later in a different circumstance. This is especially important when creating a library or a common function used across a site.

5. It is important to perform form validation on both the client side and the server side in a Web application because the client cannot be trusted to be benevolent. A client may intentionally try to inject code to break an application or take over an application. The testing on the client side is for legitimate users to enter correct information for the system to behave properly.

7. Languages like PHP and Perl can be used to send email from a server to a computer but JavaScript is not capable of generating and sending e-mail on the client side due to the control over the host system that JavaScript would have to have for this behavior. If JavaScript had this power, then it could take over a host system. PHP and Perl use the server system on which they reside to perform these tasks, leaving the user's machine out of the process.

Chapter 8

Chapter Knowledge Check

1. f
3. a
5. a
7. a
9. a

Chapter Review Questions

3. Having a common language like SQL for use across multiple commercial database systems provides standards for inter-communication of database systems and interoperability of code from one system to another. If each database system had its own query language, then it would be very difficult to transfer data from one system to another and for programming languages to interact with the database system. Web applications

would need specific code depending upon the type of database to which they are connected, which would increase development cost and limit flexibility.

5. Using SQL queries to create database tables within Web applications could cause multiple duplicate tables to be created or even a new table for each use of the application. This is a poor decision for design and it would make managing the database incredibly difficult. The system would likely become unstable as a result.

7. There are a variety of additional uses for *isset* in a Web application aside from testing whether a record is present in a MySQL result. These include testing for the presence of a variable within a form or as output from a function. This is often essential to test before using a variable that does not exist, which would cause an error on the page.

INDEX

A

Active Server Pages
   (ASP), 197, 200
Adobe Dreamweaver,
   35, 46–47, 138
Adobe Flash® object, 146
alert() function, 171
alt attribute, 71
ampersand command,
   136–137
anchor point, 86
AND operator, 179
Apple Safari, 6
argument, 162
Arial, 22

B

back-end languages, 197–198
Bitmap (BMP), 63
break statement, 167

C

Cascading Style Sheets (CSS)
   classes and tags, 81–82
   CSS3, 80
   defined, 79
   display properties, 97–107
   height and width properties,
      91–94
   IDs, 82–83
   inheritance, 84
   invoking styles in HTML,
      80–81
   layering, 89–91
   margins, 94–97
   padding, 94–97
   positioning, 84–89
   pseudo-classes, 83
   reusing of styles, 108–109
   style command, 80
   Styles Panel, 49

   Styles panel, 47
   use of, 60
character entity in HTML, 136
cloning of pages, 131–133
color choice in a page, 25–26
computational complexity, 156
conditional statements, 165–168

D

database, 228
decomposing the prototype, 58–59
default statement, 167
design set for the site, 42–44
   of Zippy Beans Coffee
      Company, case project, 45
digital typography, 22–23
display-oriented CSS
   background images, 97–99
   colors property, 99–103
   content alignment, 104
   setting borders, 103–104
   shadows property, 104–105
   text modification, 106–107
Doctype Declaration (DTD), 12–13
dollar *($)* sign, 189
Domain name registration,
   198–199
Domain Name Service (DNS), 199
do/while loop, 170
dynamic content, 179–182

E

elastic measurement, 91
e-mail accounts, 199
e-mailing
   JavaScript, 173, 175–178
   Perl, 216–218
   PHP, 208–209
embedded code, 146–147
entry, 228
equals sign *(=)* syntax, 160
escape character (), 175

date and time in, 229–230
decimal data type in, 229
graphical user Interface (GUI)
for, 230
integer specification in, 229
retrieving data from database,
240–242
storing data in database,
239–240
using with PHP, 236–242

N
Notepad++, 49–50, 108

P
padding, 94–97
page testing, 17–18
parameter, 162
PERL, 46
Perl
  basics, 211–212
  e-mailing with,
    216–218
  form processing, 212–215
PHP, 46, 228
  basics, 202–203
  e-mailing with, 208–209
  form processing, 204–207
  MySQL with, 236–242
pipe character *(|)*, 175
pixel, 23
pixels, 86
planning of Web site
  audience, 40–41
  design and development
    process, 36–38
  design set for the site, 42–44
  emphasizing and showcasing
    content, 41–42
  initial client communication,
    38–40
  purpose, 40–41
Portable Network Graphic
  (PNG), 63, 67, 69

position property of CSS, 84–89
  element position, 85–89
  setting positioning and anchor
    points, 87–89
  values, 85
PowerPoint, 125
programming language, 156
projects, chapter, 30–31,
  53, 75, 118, 150–151,
  192–193, 221, 245–246

R
relational database, 228
relational database management
  system (RDMS), 228
relationship property, 108
relative referencing, 16
Ruby on Rails, 200

S
sans-serif, 23
scope of a variable, 164
scripting language, 156
serif, 23
server-side language, 156
server-side languages, 198
server-side programming
  languages, 200
server space, 199
site icon, adding, 133–134
site layout
  decomposing a design, 58–59
  planning of functionality, 58
site layout in HTML
  method for constructing
    layouts, 60–62
  structuring a page, 60
  using HTML text, 60–62
site map, creating, 125–126
src attribute, 70–71, 127
Stanford Web Credibility
  Project, 21
Structured Query Language
  (SQL), 227
  insert queries, 236
  select queries, 234–235

update queries, 235
style commands, 80, 84
switch statement, 167

T

table, 229
Tag Image File Format (TIFF), 63
text adjustment properties
    font-family, 106
    font-size, 106
    font-style, 106
    font-weight, 106
    text-decoration, 106
    text-shadow, 106–107
Times New Roman, 22
tracking, 24
type attribute, 157
typefaces, 22

U

Uniform Resource Locator
    (URL), 1, 8–9

V

values in JavaScript
    Boolean values, 159
    character values, 159–160
    integer and decimal values,
      159
    string values, 160
variable, 156
View Selection, 47

W

Web browser, 3–6, 24, 62

common, 5–6
Webmonkey Web site
Web page, 4–6
Web pages, principles of
    color choice, 25–26
    considering purpose and
      audience, 21
    evaluation of page, 27
    page layout and real estate,
      19–20
    typography and font selection,
      22–24
Web server, 3
Web site, 3
    hosting a, 197–200
    planning of. *see* planning of
      Web site
    traffic patterns, 200
What You See Is What You Get
    (WYSIWYG) view, 47
while loop, 169
WHOIS database, 199
World Wide Web Consortium
    (W3C), 4, 8, 19
World Wide Web (WWW), 1–3
W3Schools, 80
WYSIWYG display, 4

Y

You Tube®, 147

Z

z-index property, 89–90